Languages We Live By

WRITING WITHOUT BORDERS

Writing Without Borders exists to provide space for writing and thought which challenges the norms of academic discourse. Books in the series will touch on Multilingual Matters' key themes – multilingualism, social justice and the benefits of diversity and dialogue – but need not focus entirely on them. Books should be short (20,000–40,000 words is ideal) and represent a departure in some way from what and how you would usually write a journal paper or book manuscript. They may contain experimental writing, new ways of thinking or creating knowledge, topics that are not generally addressed in academic writing, or something we haven't thought of yet... The series is a place to explore, think, challenge and create. If you are not sure if your idea is 'right' for this series, please ask us.

Writers from the Global South will be particularly welcomed and sought out, as well as writers from marginalised communities and groups within the Global North. Writers from all academic disciplines are welcome, as are experts working in non-academic settings.

Full details of all the books in this series and of all our other publications can be found on http://www.multilingual-matters.com, or by writing to Multilingual Matters, BLOCK, The Fairfax, Pithay Court, Bristol, BS1 3BN, UK.

WRITING WITHOUT BORDERS: 4

Languages We Live By

Exploring Sociolinguistic Trajectories

Katrin Ahlgren and Clara Molina

MULTILINGUAL MATTERS
Bristol • Jackson

DOI https://doi.org/10.21832/AHLGRE1625
Library of Congress Cataloging in Publication Data
A catalog record for this book is available from the Library of Congress.
Names: Ahlgren, Katrin author | Molina, Clara, author
Title: Languages We Live By: Exploring Sociolinguistic Trajectories/
    Katrin Ahlgren and Clara Molina.
Description: First edition. | Bristol; Jackson: Multilingual Matters,
    2025. | Series: Writing Without Borders: 4 | Includes bibliographical
    references and index. | Summary: "This book guides the reader through
    the use of powerful creative tools to explore personal language family
    trees, language self-portraits, and autobiographical narratives as a
    means to explore the connections of speaker repertoires, identities and
    sociolinguistic justice"—Provided by publisher.
Identifiers: LCCN 2025032217 (print) | LCCN 2025032218 (ebook) | ISBN
    9781836681618 paperback | ISBN 9781836681625 hardback | ISBN
    9781836681649 epub | ISBN 9781836681632 pdf
Subjects: LCSH: Sociolinguistics—Methodology—Popular works
Classification: LCC P40.3 .A38 2025 (print) | LCC P40.3 (ebook) | DDC
    306.44072/1—dc23/eng/20250915
LC record available at https://lccn.loc.gov/2025032217
LC ebook record available at https://lccn.loc.gov/2025032218

British Library Cataloguing in Publication Data
A catalogue entry for this book is available from the British Library.

ISBN-13: 978-1-83668-162-5 (hbk)
ISBN-13: 978-1-83668-161-8 (pbk)
ISBN-13: 978-1-83668-163-2 (pdf)
ISBN-13: 978-1-83668-164-9 (epub)

Multilingual Matters
UK: BLOCK, The Fairfax, Pithay Court, Bristol, BS1 3BN, UK.
USA: Ingram, Jackson, TN, USA.
Authorised Representative: Easy Access System Europe - Mustamäe tee 50, 10621
Tallinn, Estonia, gpsr.requests@easproject.com.

Website: https://www.multilingual-matters.com
X: Multi_Ling_Mat
Bluesky: @multi-ling-mat.bsky.social
Facebook: https://www.facebook.com/multilingualmatters
Blog: https://www.channelviewpublications.wordpress.com

The policy of Multilingual Matters/Channel View Publications is to use papers that
are natural, renewable and recyclable products, made from wood grown in
sustainable forests. In the manufacturing process of our books, and to further support
our policy, preference is given to printers that have FSC and PEFC Chain of Custody
certification. The FSC and/or PEFC logos will appear on those books where full
certification has been granted to the printer concerned.

Typeset by Techset Composition India(P) Ltd, Bangalore and Chennai, India.

This guide was produced as part of the research project "Towards a new linguistic citizenship: action research for the recognition of speakers in the Madrid educational context" (ref. PID2019-105676RB-C41/AEI/10.13039/501100011033) funded by the Spanish Ministry of Science, Innovation and Universities. The book also benefited from the collaboration of the MIRCo-UAM Interdisciplinary Research Center on Multilingualism, Discourse, and Communication (for more information, see: https://mircouam.com/en/home-2) and from Katrin Ahlgren's fellowship at the Paris Institute for Advanced Study (France) as part of the Riksbankens Jubileumsfond Chair.

EquiLing   MINISTERIO DE CIENCIA, INNOVACIÓN Y UNIVERSIDADES   AGENCIA ESTATAL DE INVESTIGACIÓN

Katrin Ahlgren (katrin.ahlgren@su.se) is affiliated with Stockholm University and Clara Molina (clara.molina@uam.es) is affiliated with Universidad Autónoma de Madrid. Both are members of the MIRCo-UAM Interdisciplinary Research Center on Multilingualism, Discourse and Communication.

Katrin Ahlgren (ORCID 0000-0002-4442-6295)
Clara Molina (ORCID 0000-0002-2862-4785)

We sincerely thank the generosity of the students and workshop participants who agreed to contribute their anonymized language-related testimonies and drawings to this volume. We are also grateful for the conversations with our research colleagues, with whom we have learned to better understand the impact of the languages we live by over a lifetime.

Ninguém nasce feito: é experimentando-nos
no mundo que nós nos fazemos.

Nobody is born made: it is by experiencing
ourselves in the world that we make ourselves.

Paulo Freire, *Política e educação*

Contents

Contents

About the authors

Katrin Ahlgren works in academic and artistic fields on questions related to languages and their ideological, ethical and aesthetic dimensions. She holds the position of Associate Professor at Stockholm University, and her research interests include linguistic and cultural diversity, multilingual creativity and arts-based research. In recognition of her literary-inspired work on poetic representations and interpretations, she has been awarded the Bernadotte Scholarship by the Swedish Academy. Recently, she has been a fellow at the Institute for Advanced Study in Paris and undertaken an artistic residency program in Fukuoka, Japan.

Clara Molina is an associate professor of English language and linguistics at Universidad Autónoma de Madrid. Her research interests focus on the overlapping fields of language variation and change, educational sociolinguistics, and language in society – with particular attention to emotion, language ideologies, and identity. She conducts educational innovation projects, most recently on language and social inequality through service learning and challenge-based learning. With extensive experience in academic governance, she currently directs a peer mentoring program among higher education lecturers at her university.

Introduction

The research project behind this book

Around the world, people face situations of marginalization, in which they lack recognition, have access to fewer opportunities, or are limited in their participation because of the languages and/or varieties they speak or do not speak. EquiLing, a participatory action research project launched to analyze the role of language in social inequality, brought together sociolinguistic researchers from officially monolingual, bilingual and trilingual regions of the Spanish state. In addition to delving into how language issues create and reinforce social inequality, EquiLing researchers set out to intervene to try to reverse processes of linguistic surveillance and discrimination.

In participatory action research, researchers accompany participants as they build a critical stance (in this case, by detecting and analyzing cases of language-related inequality) and co-construct knowledge that facilitates social change. To support this process, EquiLing developed methodological tools, such as this guide, which are designed to help speakers explore their linguistic biographies and repertoires, understand their linguistic history and recognize themselves in language. The aim is not to 'celebrate' linguistic diversity, but to use it as a lever to build fairer societies. To make this possible, we believe it is important to create safe spaces where participants can speak freely about their language-related experiences throughout their lives. When participants share such experiences with others, it facilitates understanding of the impact that languages have on themselves and others. Hence, this guide.

For more information about EquiLing, see the multilingual website with audiovisual reference materials, at: https://www.equiling.eu/en/.

Why this guide and who is it for?

Of all the injustices in the world, why pay attention to those that relate to language? Are they really that significant? With this guide, we intend to show that they are, and that linguistic injustices affect everyone. If our society sustains only one speaker model – the standard monolingual native model – we all live in an unjust environment and continue to feed a spiral of symbolic violence. If we do not give importance to the inequality that we create with language, we risk reproducing it, and the gap gets bigger and bigger.

Linguists know that all languages are equally good because each one fully meets the communicative needs of its speakers (and, if that is not the case, speakers readily adapt them so that they do). In all languages, speakers come to understand both themselves and others. Yet in everyday life, language ideologies and hierarchies place more value on certain ways of speaking, thereby giving greater prestige to some speakers over others. Thus, many end up thinking that there are languages (and language varieties) that are worth learning, while others are better left at home because they close rather than open doors.

Inspired by Paulo Freire's critical pedagogy, EquiLing has joined this debate and taken it to classrooms and citizen groups, to try and make people realize that language encapsulates much more than communication, and engage them in the development of more innovative, inclusive and responsible societies. Over recent decades, interest in language and power relations, and the ensuing legitimization of some speakers while others are misrecognized, has gradually given rise to a wave of intersectional interest in social justice. In such explorations, language is but one piece in a complex puzzle that also includes social class, age, gender, cultural and ethnic background, and more. In this enterprise, EquiLing has consistently claimed that linguists need to engage in sociolinguistic action, rather than in academic work alone. Part and parcel of this forerunner stance is the decision to create open-access resources such as this theoretical guide, aimed not only at the academic community but at anyone who wants to understand the role that language plays in our everyday lives and life experiences.

With a focus on speakers rather than on languages, this guide offers a proposal to explore the many paths that our sociolinguistic trajectories and repertoires allow. It can be used in formal and informal education, language classes, grassroots associations, and all sorts of socialization activities. We believe that the social construction of the notion of speakerhood is largely in our hands, if we learn how to investigate the languages within us. Therefore, we invite you to explore your own and others' linguistic biographies and repertoires, so that the analysis of language-related critical incidents can serve as leverage for growth.

What does the guide contain?

This guide stems from research but is not intended to provide academic results. Rather, it aims to propose strategies and tools that anyone can use to reflect on the impact of languages on our lives.

Chapter 1: Sociolinguistic trajectories

The guide starts with a reflection on how we relate to languages and the impact they have on people throughout their lifetime. To reach a wide audience, explanations of key critical sociolinguistic concepts have been included in plain language. In this first chapter, the focus is on two main concepts: linguistic biographies and linguistic repertoires. The purpose is that everyone can understand how sociolinguistic concepts help to inspect the power relations ingrained in language use and how they impact societies and individuals.

Chapter 2: Narrating life, self and language

This chapter contains brief explanations of how we can understand ourselves through storytelling, addressing communication strategies and linguistic creativity in relation to multilingualism, emotion and identity. Here it is argued that sharing real-life experiences and critical incidents through narration can help people to better appreciate themselves and others. With this knowledge, it is possible to co-create alternative stories that challenge hegemonic speaker models and foster opportunities for change.

Chapter 3: Tools for exploring linguistic biographies and repertoires

This chapter provides practical guidelines for approaching our linguistic biographies and repertoires through (i) personal language family trees, (ii) language self-portraits, and (iii) autobiographical language narratives. These tools are not new; similar approaches have been used before in different educational contexts around the world. However, we present examples of how EquiLing researchers have used them in hands-on seminars, sometimes in one language, often in several. By sharing these examples, we want to help people realize that all their languages are valuable resources and to initiate critical reflections.

Chapter 4: Workshop proposal

The guide includes a proposal on how to use the tools described in Chapter 3. It is offered as an indication only, since we encourage users to adapt the tools to their purposes, and the contexts and the people who will use them. We believe, in any case, that the best way to work with the tools is collaboratively, as the very act of sharing language-related experiences in small group constellations is eye-opening.

Chapter 5: To learn more

At the end, this guide includes a glossary with brief explanations of some of the theoretical concepts addressed throughout the text. This chapter also includes references to relevant publications by the EquiLing team and to other scholars who have explored similar topics and tools.

1 Sociolinguistic trajectories

Languages We Live By

Languages shape our lives from the moment we are born until our final days. They are not just means of expression and interaction but also gateways to different viewpoints and beliefs. The languages we acquire, use and evolve with throughout our lives deeply influence the way we think and relate to ourselves, others, and the world around us. Some of us grow up with a single language, but most do with several languages or linguistic varieties. Although this may seem surprising, the truth is that monolingualism is an exception, whereas multilingualism is and has always been the norm throughout the world. This is even more true today because, with increasing global mobility, many people live with multiple languages at home, at work and in everyday life.

- Can you think of a family scenario where one parent speaks to their children in one language, the other parent uses a different one, and all of them also speak a third language?
- Do you know someone who speaks one language at home and another one at work or school?

- Have you heard people using one language variety in the place where they live and a different one when they visit relatives in the hometown where they are originally from?

In multilingual families, as well as in other multilingual settings, translanguaging (that is, using all the languages and varieties in one's repertoire) is very common. From the outside, this switching and mixing of linguistic resources may seem confusing, but it comes naturally to bilingual and multilingual people. It is a creative use of language that reflects the rich hybridity of identities, creates bonds and helps overcome communicative barriers.

While learning a new language can be a conscious choice and a pleasure for some, it can also be an obligatory duty for others, often related to the national education system or labor market requirements. For people who experience displacement – voluntarily or not – learning a new language is often mandatory. Many Western countries have enforced language requirements for citizenship, and competence in a national language has often been pointed out in the political debate as key for 'integration' as well as for establishing and maintaining social networks and participating in community life. However, since people who learn a language in adulthood may not be able to achieve 'full proficiency' in the dominant language of the host society, they run the risk of never being considered legitimate speakers or even full members of society. This may also be the case for people belonging to disadvantaged communities, who for various reasons do not manage to keep up with standard varieties.

Speaker legitimacy is also at play when different languages come in contact with each other, as some tend to enjoy a higher status than others. This is something that happens all the time. One tangible example is the case of English, considered a lingua franca in large parts of the world, a common language for people who share no other means of communication. Speaking English enables many communicative exchanges that would not otherwise be possible and facilitates international travel, economic transactions, scientific collaboration, and cultural exchange. For this reason, it has often been ideologically linked to success in society, and learning English is often considered an investment expected to pay off in social and economic capital. Still, its hegemonic dominance raises concerns about linguistic homogenization and the marginalization of local languages and cultures – leading to critical debates about linguistic diversity and cultural preservation. For millions of speakers around the world English is an opportunity, because it allows access to huge amounts of content. But, at the same time, it is also a disadvantage for those whose first language is not English, as many resources that might have been accessible to them in their own language are no longer so.

Moreover, when we think of English, we tend to think of one, two, or three varieties at most, usually tied to a national standard (American, British, Canadian, etc.). However, there are many situations in which people use forms of English that do not conform to any of those norms and do not have much to do with standardized language tests. In all these cases, a conflict arises between the supposed neutrality of English (since it belongs to no one, it belongs to everyone) and the benchmarks used to categorize speakers as legitimate or not. These and other situations in which language functions as a gatekeeper, aggravating inequalities and helplessness among speakers, have been an object of inquiry in critical sociolinguistics. Adopting a critical stance involves examining how language use changes in different social contexts and how it reflects cultural norms, power dynamics and the construction of our identities. A critical perspective also entails reflecting on language policies, minority language education and multilingualism.

The benefits of multilingualism have often been highlighted. Researchers have shown that speaking several languages not only enhances cognitive flexibility but also broadens cultural perspectives and improves social skills. Moreover, it has been argued that people who are proficient in multiple languages often exhibit greater problem-solving abilities and creativity and are even better equipped to maintain their memory as they age. However, multilingualism is not always socially welcome. One need only recall the biblical story of Babel, in which human beings were punished by having each one speaking a different language and thus condemned to not understand each other. Today, many beliefs that reject multilingual and non-standard language practices persist. For instance, in

Language and surveillance often come together

many schools, mixing languages is not permitted, and languages must be kept separate even though, within each of us, all our resources for languaging (that is, using verbal and non-verbal communication to create meaning) form a single, integrated repertoire.

- What would it take to reverse negative conceptions of linguistic diversity?
- Would a 'happy Babel' be possible where all human languages coexisted side by side and were used without conflict or hierarchical boundaries?
- What could be the consequences of such an ideological change?

Linguistic intolerance is also the reason why some languages are regarded as valuable and therefore worth learning, investing time and money in, while others are relegated to the domestic sphere, rather than used in public or official domains. The main problem is that, when we categorize languages hierarchically, we are not only ranking languages but also speakers. It does not make much sense to think people are better or worse because of how they speak, but it happens. On those occasions, languages become tools of repression and symbolic violence, and this has serious consequences for those who are despised for not speaking 'properly'. Those who are stigmatized because of how they sound can be denied the opportunity to rent an apartment, for example, while someone else with a more 'neutral' accent may be prioritized. Or they can be refused access to a job for which they are qualified because their accent is perceived as 'small town' or 'chav'. Or they can be harassed or rejected for sounding 'queer'. In a globalized world where borders are more and more liquid, countless testimonies of people with experience of migration (even second- or third-generation migrants) report feeling watched at every interaction and being asked repeatedly where they are from. Because, as language is embodied – not an isolated mental process, but intertwined with our physical body, our movements and our sensory experiences – belonging (that is, being and feeling 'one of us') is not within everyone's reach.

This is why, in critical sociolinguistic research with a social justice perspective, there is a great interest in how individuals relate to their language learning and language use over a life span. Two concepts frequently used to explore people's life stories with a focus on language are linguistic biographies and linguistic repertoires – both imply taking the individual speaker as a point of departure to gain a better understanding of the existential and embodied dimensions of language use and how it varies and changes over time.

Linguistic biographies

In sociolinguistic research, narrative accounts that focus on how language(s) shapes our life trajectories are called linguistic biographies. These narratives can be told or written, individually or collectively, in formal or informal language. Sometimes they can take the form of collages or multimodal fanzines with images, sounds and short texts. The only limit to their format is our imagination, and the only requirement is to think about how, as we navigate through life, our linguistic biographies evolve alongside our life trajectories. This can be done by tracing our language choices (whether intended or unintended), describing how we learn and use languages over time, as well as taking note of our emotions, strategies and coping mechanisms. When we analyze what our language choices reveal about our sense of self and belonging, we can delve deeper into our self-perceptions and identities.

The relationship between linguistic biographies and life trajectories, however, is intricate and sometimes hard to track, as languages do not only reflect our personal experiences but also our cultural environment. Language is always situated in a social context, which is why language-related anecdotes can provide a wealth of information about the surrounding society, language ideologies, people's attitudes toward different varieties and languages, as well as educational and institutional regulations.

Therefore, when analyzing sociolinguistic trajectories, we should always question the reasons for the patterns of language variation that we observe, that is, how language differs depending on the context in which it is used. This variability gives rise to different registers, dialects and sociolects (and, of course, to many hybridization practices). We should also track patterns of language change in our repertoire, that is, how our language use and competencies differ over time and to what extent such changes are influenced by education, career, friends, family constellations, travel, migration, or exposure to new environments. Examining language use (how we speak, write, or sign in different circumstances, such as at home, in school, with friends, at work, and within social networks) with all its nuances and contradictions also allows us to examine significant aspects of language acquisition and socialization (how, where, with whom, and for what purposes we as individuals learn, and acquire, languages, whether it is our first language(s) or additional ones acquired later in life).

Exploring sociolinguistic trajectories can sometimes seem like entering a labyrinth, as they encompass movements across time and space that involve both formal and informal learning and use, including online and offline experiences, as well as language practices that are sometimes real and sometimes imagined. However, the maze is worth the struggle, because reconstructing linguistic biographies helps us gain insight into the complex interplay between language and individual development across our lifespan, shedding light on how language shapes and is shaped by our vital trajectories. Narrative accounts with a focus on language also provide insights into asymmetrical power relations in society and linguistic discrimination, both overt and hidden. Conclusively, linguistic biographies can include some or all the languages we have in our linguistic repertoires, languages we speak freely or only understand a little of, as well as languages we have repressed, forgotten, or want to learn in the future.

Linguistic repertoires

Within a speech community, the notion of linguistic repertoire refers to all the languages, varieties and registers used by the members of the collective – as well as how they are distributed (almost always

The linguistic repertoire of multilinguals, an integrated whole of resources

hierarchically) in a given sociolinguistic space. The notion is also used to refer to the whole set of linguistic skills and resources that a person possesses, with either active or passive competence. Some people, for instance, may be able to speak a language, but not write it. Or they can understand while they listen to someone else, but not speak in that language, or not fluently. In this guide, it is such personal linguistic repertories that are in focus.

Everyone has an individual repertoire of language resources that they use for different purposes, and that changes throughout their lives:

- Think of the languages you have learned or forgotten ever since you were born.
- Reflect on the languages you can recognize and those you would like to speak in the future.
- Think about the languages you wish you had learned as a child, or that you abandoned and now wish you had not.
- Consider the languages and varieties you are proud or ashamed of, and when, where, or who you use(d) them with.
  That is the impact of your linguistic repertoire on your life!

The notion of linguistic repertoire has been explored in depth in sociolinguistic research and has somewhat undermined more traditional views of language competence. Thus, some researchers argue that, rather than thinking of languages as distinct entities and focusing on the level of proficiency achieved in standardized tests in each of them, we should rather pay attention to the conglomerate of communicative resources and strategies available to a person, which includes linguistic, extra-linguistic, social and cultural knowledge and skills that complement each other in various ways. All those resources are part of a single, indivisible whole in the same way that tributary streams joining a river flow into a single unified current. Therefore, many argue that language mixing should not be penalized, but rather speakers should be encouraged to express themselves using all the resources at their disposal (not only those linked to a specific language or variety, often the hegemonic one, to which not everyone has access). However, other researchers question the benefits of translanguaging (while valuing linguistic repertoires as tools that facilitate language learning, communication and social belonging) and believe that the boundaries between languages and varieties should be preserved.

In any case, when examining our linguistic repertoires, we must keep in mind that our skills are never the same in all the languages we speak. And in any given context we will feel more or less comfortable in one language than in others. This is perfectly fine because we never use all languages in all contexts: in some, for example, we will only talk about intimate stuff, while in others we will only write about formal matters. Therefore, as language skills are always in transition and we are all learners to some extent, it does not make sense to draw a rigid boundary between native and non-native speakers, or between born and emergent bilinguals. It makes more sense to become aware of the fluency, accuracy, persuasiveness and rapport with which we can communicate in different languages or contexts. And, if possible, to try and expand our linguistic repertoire, and improve our awareness of it.

We must also remember that not only languages but also varieties and accents are part of our repertoire. The registers with which we address others often depend on whether we are speaking in public, chatting with friends, writing academic papers, or posting messages on social media, whether we are addressing someone in our family, a stranger, one of our colleagues or our boss, someone young or an older person. The broader our linguistic repertoire, the better we will be able to adapt to communicative situations with interlocutors from different social classes, educational levels, age ranges and geographical backgrounds. The better we understand and recognize the advantages of our linguistic repertoire, the better we will be able to use it in everyday life.

2 Narrating life, self and language

Autobiographical narration and critical incidents

In telling our life story, we more or less consciously choose to highlight different aspects, and we remember and interpret things differently throughout our lives. Time is always an important factor in story-telling. While giving an account of the trajectory of our life we are in the present, but we may be referring simultaneously to the past and the future, sometimes even to an imagined past or future, and most often we do not account for things in chronological order. Despite these leaps in time, many narratives are composed in a similar way: an introduction (who, when, what, where?), one or several high moments (what happened then?), a turning point (so what?), and finally, a resolution (what happened in the end?) with a coda signaling the conclusion of the story.

Narrations shape events and anecdotes into meaningful experiences. When we narrate our lives, we navigate and negotiate our biographical choices, challenges and opportunities about what has happened to us. We sometimes present ourselves as people with agency who take actions and steer our lives in distinctive directions, sometimes as people to whom things happen. Therefore, narratives should always be seen as constructions, especially since they can sometimes spring from

rather vague memories and can always be constructed differently. Besides, situational and rela-
tional factors always interfere when we tell stories.
Philosophers have argued that narration is a way
for us to create ourselves, meaning that we create
our identity in the act of narrating our lives.

In our research, we observed that when people
are asked to discuss their life paths in relation to
their linguistic repertoires, it becomes clear that
language is an important part of everything we do.
However, most people are unaware of how they
speak, why they adapt their language to others, or
how they shift from one register to another.
Therefore, narrating our lives in relation to language can help us understand ourselves better.
Sometimes, such narratives even have a therapeu-
tic, healing function, because they help us understand critical linguistic incidents in our lives,
situations in which our way of speaking had an
impact on us, and that remain etched in our minds
because of the strong emotions they mobilized.
Verbalizing such critical incidents can not only
trigger self-understanding, but also empathy from
others, and sometimes even a collective desire for
change. When several people critically examine
language-related incidents and realize that a lan-
guage-mediated situation is unfair, they can create
counter-narratives to resist linguistic discrimination and foster a more inclusive sociolinguistic
order that challenges existing social hierarchies
and speaker models (that is, all those idealizations
that are reinforced in the collective imagination –
such as the 'standard' speaker, the 'native' speaker,
the 'neutral' speaker – to which we often aspire,

but which very rarely happen in real life). The notion of speakerhood (the social construction of what it means to be a 'good' speaker of a language) and its various ramifications (new speakers who learn a language later in life, emerging bilinguals with hybrid linguistic practices, multilingual learners, etc.) is becoming increasingly relevant in sociolinguistics, due to the multiple crossovers of language ideologies and social processes.

Communication strategies and multilingual creativity

In this theoretical guide, participants are invited to use different communication styles – spoken, written and visual elements such as drawings and pictures. Since the guide can be used in different contexts, with speakers of different backgrounds and linguistic competencies, the outcomes will differ from case to case. Some participants may have the habit of reasoning in abstract terms or may be familiar with the field of (socio)linguistics. For others, this may be the first time they have encountered critical theoretical concepts. Or maybe the difference comes from their age and life experiences: think of a teenager in a city versus a mother in the countryside or an elderly man in a continent far away from the place he was born. However, we believe that a critical stance fosters creativity, and that everyone can benefit from reflection on life and language.

A useful strategy for speakers who find it difficult to talk about abstract notions is to 'talk in images'. It can thus be beneficial for the participants in a sociolinguistic trajectories activity to be reminded about the possibility of using imaginative language. When we cannot find a particular word to express an abstract concept, it is always possible to describe it metaphorically. Far from being a rhetorical device used only by poets, metaphors are powerful ways of conceptualizing reality that are used by everyone, not least by people who are learning to speak a new language. In fact, we are often unaware that we conceptualize in metaphorical ways all the time, such as, for instance, when we say 'life is a journey' or 'learning a language is hard work' without noticing the underlying images. Some researchers in cognitive linguistics even argue that our whole conception of the word is metaphorically constructed, so conceptual metaphors not only shape speech, but also the way we think and act.

In the mediatic discourse on language, especially from a migration perspective, there is an oft-quoted metaphor: 'language is the key to society'. Another ubiquitous metaphor explains why diseases are often conceived of in terms of war: 'We were fighting COVID'. Such images, which speak volumes about the way our society thinks, are often presented as unquestioned truth, but we can consciously try to detect them, then critically discuss them, or even avoid them altogether if they turn out to be harmful conceptualizations. At other times, metaphors can express humor (for example, if we talk about language use as 'a soccer game, in which every word is a pass, and together they create an exciting game of communication') or they can be poetic (such as when we talk about using a new language 'fluently' and the feeling of 'flying like a bird, high in the sky'). The images used by speakers in their autobiographical language narratives – whether they are day-to-day and well-known or inventive and creative – can tell us a lot about their values and beliefs, and how they feel about themselves and their languages.

The notion of linguistic creativity in relation to second language and multilingual speakers is complex since it is related to linguistic conventions, and whether deviation from standardized norms is considered as an 'error' or as resourcefulness. Linguistic creativity is thus interrelated to who is deemed a legitimate 'owner' of the language, a valid interlocutor who can introduce innovations. Moreover, the creativity that defies linguistic norms is particularly intriguing in the case of translanguaging, when speakers fluently mix all the languages in their repertoire and play with words, sounds, grammar and even metaphors. Such multilingual creativity contributes to the creation of self and identity.

Language, emotion and identity

Intuitively, everyone agrees there is a link between language and identity. However, identity is a very complex, intersectional notion that relates to many categories, some intertwined and some not, such as nationality, ethnicity, gender and class. Even our age, our occupation, and our likes and dislikes have to do with our identity. The crossovers are so numerous that it is hard to explain what the connection is between our language and who we are.

Those who have studied linguistics know that we do not speak a language (because no one speaks the whole of a language), but an idiolect. That is, the very particular way each of us has of expressing ourselves, our very personal communicative style: the words that we use, our grammar choices, how we pronounce words, the accent we have, and so on. Idiolects are always an amalgam that never coincides 100% with any of the 'named languages' of the world.

True, when asked, we say we speak English, Spanish, Swedish, or any of the more than 6,000 languages spoken around the world. We tend to feel attached to that language and, sometimes, we even recognize 'our language' when we see a flag. But if you think about it, this univocal relationship between a language and a nation does not make sense, even if we are used to it. Why not? Because with less than 200 countries in the world, more than 6,000 languages, and over 8 million people, the math does not add up. Unlike states, which are often monolingual and even have an official language, almost everyone in the world is multilingual. And of course, no one person has an official language. What we do have is one or several languages, varieties and registers that, together, make up our linguistic repertoire.

Our linguistic repertoire is linked to our identities, as it reflects the places we have lived in, the people we have interacted with, the things that interest us, the networks in which we socialize, and so on. Our personal experiences shape our linguistic repertoires and these, in turn, influence how others perceive us, and also how we perceive ourselves. This leads to the question: How do our linguistic repertoires influence our self-perception?

- Think of how some people react physically to foreign-sounding speakers, for instance, on public transport.
- Think of decisions made based on how others speak or write, for instance, when responding to a post in a dating app or a job application.
- Think of feelings, such as shame, fear, or frustration, that have often been linked to language use, or excitement, joy and pride too.

By paying attention to embodied dimensions of language use, it is possible to better understand how language, emotion and identity are related. It can also help us observe turning points related to critical life junctures – whether by choice or not (such as a new school, a new job opportunity, a new partner, or a move to a new country) that could lead to significant shifts in language use or attitude toward language. Let us now explore how to do this.

3 Tools for exploring linguistic biographies and repertoires

To investigate the 'languages we live by', this guide proposes three tools with which to explore our linguistic biographies and repertoires:

(i) Personal language family trees
(ii) Language self-portraits
(iii) Autobiographical language narratives

For each tool, an explanation of what it consists of is followed by a discussion of why it is relevant, along with a description of how it has been used by EquiLing members and how it can be explored together with other people.

(i) Personal language family trees

Language family trees have a long tradition in linguistics. Since the 19th century, trees have been used to display the origins and relationships between genetically related languages (such as those comprising the Indo-European family, which includes over 400 languages spoken by 3 billion people throughout Europe and the northern Indian subcontinent, as well as many former colonies across the globe; or the Niger-Congo family, which includes almost 1400 languages spoken by more than 600 million people in Africa). However, when speakers trace their personal language family tree, they are not seeking to trace language families. Instead, they are mapping the languages spoken by themselves, their parents, grandparents and other relatives. Such diachronic language mapping is significant because it allows learning about what has happened to somebody's kin by means of tracing the languages spoken in their family throughout the generations.

To display how this tool has and can be explored, several examples will be presented. The first one comes from Flor, a graduate student from Peru. At the time she drew this personal language family tree, she was in Madrid taking a course in sociolinguistics as part of a master's degree in applied linguistics. English was the language of instruction for the degree, which hosted students from around the world who had majored in language studies and were interested in global communication.

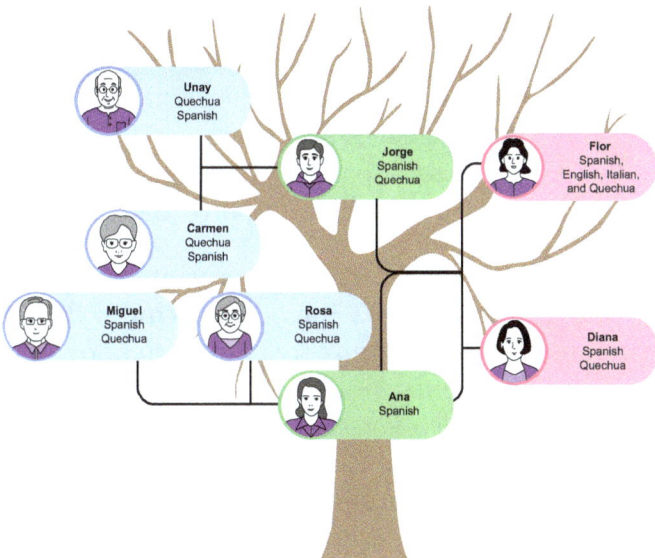

Flor's personal language family tree

As you can see, Flor's grandparents on her mother's side spoke Spanish as their first language and also Quechua. On her father's side, the languages were the same, but in a different order: Quechua was their first language and Spanish came second. That is probably why Flor's dad speaks Quechua (and has passed it on to his daughters, Flor and her sister) but her mum does not. So, the only family language they all share is Spanish. The tree reflects the colonial history of the Latin American continent, and how it has affected languages (many of which are now minoritized, gravely endangered, or extinct) and language transmission over generations. Notice as well how personal choices are also important: Flor learned two other languages, English and Italian, whereas her sister did not. If you were to guess:

- Why do you think she chose those two languages?
- What does the order in which she lists her languages mean?
- What role do you think Quechua plays in the sisters' relation to their dad?

The example that follows was created by Beiye, a young woman from China. By looking at Beiye's personal language family tree we get to know that her grandparents not only spoke Mandarin Chinese, but also Russian. We can also see that her parents did not learn Russian, but English. And Beiye, in addition to English, also learned Spanish. This tells us about geopolitical relations and about which languages are hegemonic at a

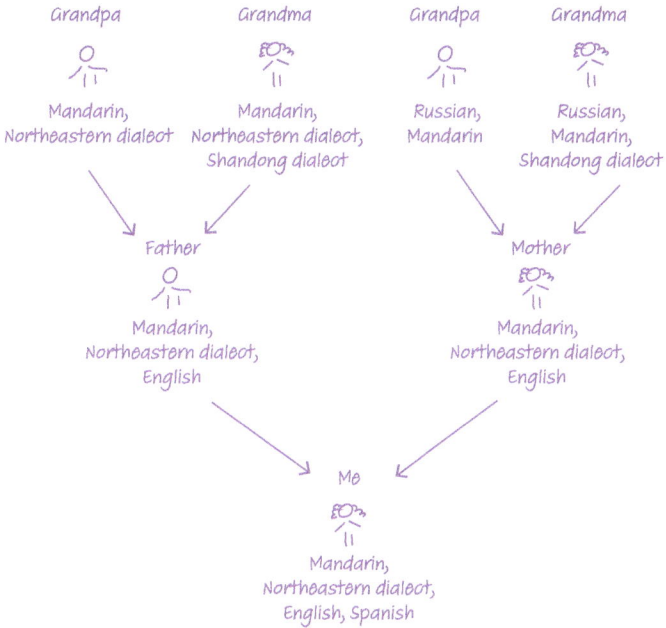

Beiye's personal language family tree

given place and time. If we look closely at the dialects spoken by the members of this family, we realize that, besides Mandarin Chinese, some speak the northeastern dialect, others the Shandong dialect (on the east coast of China, but further south), and some both. This tells us about internal migrations and about language policies. Still, many questions arise when looking at this drawing, some of which could be explored by interviewing family members. Their answers would allow us to know:

— Why doesn't her grandfather speak any other dialects? Has he always lived in the place where he was born? How long did he attend school and what was the language of instruction at that time?

— Why did her grandmother learn Russian? Did she travel abroad or was it common to learn this language when she was young? What was the reason for this?

— Why did her mum learn English instead of Russian? Where and how did she learn it?

Below you will find more questions you can ask yourself before you sketch your own tree to record all the languages, dialects and/or varieties spoken in your family (perhaps your parents and grandparents will be enough):

- What languages do you speak? What varieties and dialects?
- How many languages can you recognize even if you do not know them?
- Is there any language you can read but not speak? Or the other way round?
- Is there any language that you used to speak but have forgotten? How did that happen? Do you regret it, or do you really not care?
- Is there any language you wish your parents had taught you? Why didn't they?
- At school, why did you learn English (or whatever language you learned) instead of another language? Did you choose for yourself or did your family or school decide for you? Are you happy with this choice? Why? Why not?

Once you have traced your own language family tree, interviews with relatives can help understand some of the whys and wherefores:

- Why do your relatives speak (whatever language/variety) at home instead of any other?
- Are there any languages they were forced to learn, or forbidden to speak, at some point?
- How do they feel about the different languages in their repertoires? How do these repertoires reflect their life choices?

There are so many questions you can ask yourself and others about languages in the family. Feel free to expand the list with additional questions!

(ii) Language self-portraits

Language self-portraits are visual representations that illustrate the embodied linguistic resources of speakers. Often, they can help to visualize the symbolic meaning of languages and linguistic varieties. This is why they have been used in sociolinguistic research as a methodological tool to promote language awareness and to illustrate linguistic resources among multilingual speakers (particularly among children at school) or to generate conversations that reveal power relations and language ideologies (mainly with international students and/or adults with migration backgrounds).

The starting point for a linguistic self-portrait can be a prefabricated, empty body silhouette in which speakers are invited to draw their languages in different colors. Or it can be a blank white paper (or computer file) for participants to start from scratch, draw a full body portrait of themselves, and fill it with colors that represent their different linguistic resources. Keep in mind that colors are often related to emotions; think, for example, of how advertising takes advantage of these associations, which, let's not forget, are culturally conditioned. Consequently, the same color can have very different meanings in different parts of the world.

While language portraits often speak for themselves, inviting the observer to interpret and make sense of the drawings, they can also be used as prompts that trigger narrative explanations (orally or in writing) of what each element and color in the portrait means. These visual representations can also be used for group discussions about language norms and ideologies, as well as how the different languages shape speakers' self-images. Occasionally, the portraits can depict the context in which someone uses the languages and/or varieties they know, with whom, and what each of those language forms means to the speaker.

In the participatory action research carried out by EquiLing members, linguistic self-portrayal has resulted in colorful and imaginative visual representations of speakers' linguistic repertoires, drawn by hand or digitally. This first portrait comes from Bo (a classmate of the students whose family language tree we saw in the personal family tree section).

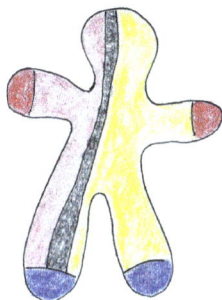

● Spanish ● Japanese ● English
● Dongyang dialect   ● Mandarin

Bo's language portrait

In her portrait, Bo has drawn a simple body sil-houette and filled it in with different colors, one for each of the languages she speaks. We can see that she is a multilingual person, and that she marks two of these languages as her 'mother tongues' (Dongyang dialect and Mandarin).

When Bo explains her language portrait, she says that she speaks the Dongyang dialect (a city in the Yangtze River Delta in northeastern China) with her grandparents, since it is the only language they all have in common. She also uses it with friends in her hometown and with her parents, although all of them speak Mandarin as well as 'dialect'. She clarifies that Mandarin Chinese is 'the language that comes from inside even some-times without thinking', probably because it is the one used in schools and in which people all over the country communicate. That explains why she has put it (in yellow) in a large part of her body silhouette.

Note that one of Bo's 'mother tongues' is a dialect. This is not a mistake. It is rather a realistic way of depicting language use. Because, not only in China but everywhere, there is no infallible way to distinguish a language from a dialect. Many people believe that the difference between a language and a dialect is that people who speak different languages cannot understand each other, but people who speak different dialects can. This is not true: in China, it often happens that speakers of different 'dialects' (which can have millions of speakers each) do not understand each other. And the opposite can also happen. In some northern European countries, such as Norway and Sweden, speakers can understand each other even though they speak different languages. Because, in fact, the difference between 'language' and 'dialect' is political and historical, rather than linguistic. That is why it has been said that 'a language is a dialect with a navy and an army'. Sometimes people mistakenly think that dialects and varieties are less important than languages, but that is not true. The truth is that we all speak dialect!

In addition to her local dialect and Mandarin (which, in fact, as any other standard language, is yet another dialect, although it enjoys more recognition and status), Bo speaks English, and she uses this language to communicate with people all over the world on the internet. She also speaks Spanish, but she says she feels clumsy in this language: that is why, in her drawing, she has placed Spanish (in blue) on her feet. Japanese, a language in which she watches anime and feels a little more confident, has been placed in her hands (colored in red). Why? Because hands allow us to do many things, and Japanese is a 'tool' for Bo which allows her to do things.

Now take a look at Bo's portrait again:

- Why do you think each language occupies the position and surface it does?
- Why do you think she started the list with Spanish, even though this is the language in which she feels less confident?
- We already know why Spanish and Japanese are on her feet and hands, but how would you explain the placement of the rest of the languages she speaks?
- What do the colors she used in her drawing mean to you? Can you associate any of those colors with any emotions?

Another example comes from Tekle, a man living in Sweden, originally from Eritrea. After drawing his self-portrait (see following page), a body dressed in vivid colors, Tekle explains the significance of each language in his life. This is how we learned that Swedish is placed in his head since 'foreigners' like him must 'think a lot when they talk'. The head is colored red because Swedes get easily burned in the sun. He says also that he considers himself as a Swede now after many years

Svenska
Tigrinya
Amhare
Engleska
Italianska

Tekle's language portrait

in the country. Further, he refers to Tigrinya (a language spoken in northeast Africa) as his roots,
placing this language at the feet. The feet are black,
representing the 'dark skin' of the people in his
country. 'These are people who regularly walk
barefoot', he says (since the weather permits it),
and are often poor (shoes are expensive).

The other languages he speaks are Amharic
(the official language of the neighboring country
Ethiopia) and English (which he learned in high
school). He refers to these languages as 'useful
clothes' (a yellow sweater and green pants) that can
be put on and off when needed. The hands of the
portrait are painted blue. Tekle remarks that his
'fingers are Italian' since the Italians (Eritrea was
an Italian colony from 1890–1947) are good
'manual workers', something he claims to have
inherited from his father, as well as some words
and phrases in Italian. For Tekle, the colors in this
portrait do not symbolize feelings and emotions,
but a more practical, cultural reality.

As shown in the samples above, the creativity unleashed by locating language-related experiences in different parts of the body can give way to other dimensions, helping speakers make sense of their embodied multilingual resources, trigger reflection on critical incidents in their lives, and connect with their emotions. Moreover, if shared and discussed with others, linguistic self-portraits can trigger empathy and foster a desire for sociolinguistic transformation.

To conclude this chapter, further examples of language portraits (on this occasion, from teenagers in Sweden) are provided as an invitation to consider the aesthetic and reflexive creativity of young speakers with migration backgrounds.

Language portraits drawn by teenagers

Translation of text in the drawings:

in my brain there is Swahili	Spanish	Swedish
and in my heart there is Lingala	Russian	Chinese
Swedish is in my pocket	English	Arabic

- Can you try to explain what these language self-portraits mean?
- How do you understand the colors and symbols in the portraits?
- What would your portrait look like if you did it using technology instead of handwriting? And what if you could include any other medium, such as audio or video?

It is also important to remember that linguistic repertoires are never static: they change over time, as our lives change. So, if you compare your linguistic portrait with one you might have drawn as a child or one you might draw years from now, there may be significant differences. To get you started, here are some questions to help you draw your portrait:

- What language(s), varieties and dialects do you use in your daily interactions?
- Where would you place them in your body?
- What color do you want to use for each language, and why those colors?
- Do you speak, write or understand any other languages? Maybe some dialects or varieties that do not have an 'official name'?
- Are there any languages you are learning, but have not yet mastered? Any languages you want to learn in the future?
- How could you represent all those languages, varieties and dialects?

Note that, sometimes, when drawing their portraits, people include symbolic cultural artifacts, like the flag in the hand of the girl in the pink dress. But remember that the identification of languages and nations can be problematic. Think about what flag is used to represent any specific country, Spain for instance. Then try to answer the following questions:

- How many speakers of Spanish are there in Spain?
- How many speakers of Spanish are there in the world?
- Which country in the world has the most Spanish speakers?
- With which flag is that country usually represented?
- In Spain, how many languages are there besides Spanish?

And let's think about your first language:

- Is it only used in one country?
- Is it represented by only one flag or several?
- Do all the inhabitants in your country speak only this language or other languages as well?
- Do all citizens identify with the flag that represents that language?

(iii) Autobiographical language narratives

Autobiographical language narratives are personal accounts of our lives in which our experiences of language serve as a connecting thread. Exploring the relevance of language-related events helps us visualize the symbolic meaning of languages and linguistic varieties. This narrative form permits us to chronicle our lives by focusing on language learning and experiences of language use during a particular period or throughout our whole life. In such narratives, we can also examine the languages and varieties we encounter in different contexts, reflecting on how they shape our social interactions and identity construction. Creating a comprehensive autobiographical language narrative involves asking questions about our linguistic journey, including exposure to different languages and varieties in situations of all sorts:

— Languages learned at home and at school
— Languages and varieties used in different social contexts
— Experiences of travel to places where different languages are spoken
— Migration and/or longer periods abroad which include exposure to new linguistic environments
— Sociocultural, professional and technological influences

In fact, all those moments in our lives when language has had an impact on who we are can be included and explored narratively. By intimately intertwining our life experiences with our linguistic repertoire, language narratives often result in personal accounts of our upbringings, schooling and working life. Frequently, they also include personal anecdotes and reflections about situations when language has played a crucial role. As such, they can provide insights into the multifaceted relationship of language and the construction of identities, illustrating how linguistic skills can evolve in response to familial, cultural, educational, professional, travel and migratory influences and how language use is perceived in different contexts.

In workshops conducted by EquiLing members, the participants were encouraged to make their own choices of which key moments of their language socialization, adaptation and change they wanted to highlight. Beforehand, they had been introduced to concepts and vocabulary highlighted in this guide and asked to focus on critical incidents – situations when they had experienced marginalization, or privilege, because of the way they speak, or when they had felt vulnerable, or empowered, because of their language use. We believe these moments can raise critical awareness and be a catalyst to try and change the prevailing status quo of sociolinguistic injustices. However, it is also important to highlight significant positive experiences in relation to language use.

If you traced a personal language tree previously, or drew a language self-portrait, your language narrative can comment on them. This is what Enrique did to tell the story of his life, his family, and their migration journey.

At home
Colombian Spanish
with my parents

Castillian-Colombian Spanish blend
with my brother

At the university
English
Castillian Spanish
some Turkish

With friends
English
Turkish
Castillian Spanish
"Spanglish" & "Turkenglish"

Online
English
Turkish
Castillian Spanish
some Portuguese

"Spanglish" & "Turkenglish"

Spanish
(Colombian & Castillian)
English
Turkish
some Portuguese

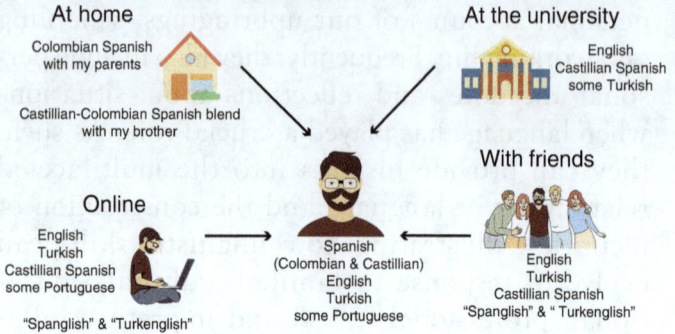

My mind is English and Spanish
Most of my thoughts are in Spanish or English

My heart is Turkish and English
Most of my emotions are expressed
through those two languages

My legs are English and Turkish
They help me to move through many different places

Enrique started his narrative as follows:

To better understand my linguistic repertoire and my
sketches, we need a little bit of context.

He continued:

I was born a long time ago in the third most populated
city of Colombia, Cali. My parents and my grandparents
are Colombians. When we, my brother and I, were very
young our parents decided to immigrate to Spain. I was
around 8-9 years old when I arrived to Madrid. The first
days I felt lost, but when I started school, I got integrated really well. However, at the beginning I had many
issues with my accent, or the variety of Spanish that I
spoke. Especially a teacher who always insisted that I

should speak 'correct Spanish'. In the variety spoken in the region where I come from, we use 'vos' and 'usted', we never use 'tú'. So, for a quite long time I tried to adapt 'my Spanish' to the context where I was, not only to sound more natural, but also because the pressure that specific teacher put on me. She was constantly forcing me to correct my Spanish.

When I started high school, I already spoke like a local, and it was at that time that I started to develop my passion for languages. When we had our first full class in English, I felt so amazed that I started paying a lot of attention and tried to learn as much as I could. It was the only class I enjoyed, and probably the only one in which I was more than average. Therefore, during my high school years I used two main languages, British English during our English classes and Spanish, Castilian Spanish with my classmates, and at home, I used Colombian Spanish.

When I was around 15-16, our parents bought a computer for us to do our homework. It was the first time I had access to a new world of opportunities. It was the first time I could access information, music, videos, etc. in English from my living room. That was when I started to have a closer contact with the English language, mainly through 'videoclips with lyrics', and videos that helped me to improve my vocabulary and pronunciation. I would say that is one of the reasons why my accent sounds more 'American' than 'British', because most of the bands, interviews, etc. that I used to listen were American.

During my last year at high school, I started meeting people online and made many friends from around the world. I used to practice my English with them through messenger and sometimes we video called each other. We talked mainly about music, football or culture, nothing interesting, but it helped me a lot to improve my English and my interest for other languages. It was during this period that I started being interested in the Turkish language. When I was 17-years old I had the opportunity to do an exchange in Turkey and meet some of my online friends. During that summer I practiced my English a lot, it was my first time abroad using English in a real context. It was also the time when I decided to learn Turkish.

As shown in my linguistic repertoire sketch, nowadays I would say that I speak fluent Spanish, English and Turkish. I use the three languages every day. Additionally, I decided to include Colombian Spanish because it is the variety my brother and I speak at home with our parents. However, when we are talking to each other, the variety we speak is a blend of Castilian Spanish with Colombian Spanish, where Castilian Spanish intonation is used but with 'seseo' [lisp] and many Colombian Spanish words and expressions. To be honest, I don't think we do this consciously, it just comes up naturally and makes our conversation flow smoother. I think it is one of the ways we use to connect with our 'Colombian' identity. As immigrants we are constantly dealing with identity, and I think speaking with my parents and my brother in Colombian Spanish is a way to preserve part of our identity.

Also, in my linguistic repertoire I included 'Spanglish' (Spanish-English blend) and 'Turkenglish' (Turkish-English blend) because they are 'languages' that I use every single day to talk to my friends, especially online. For instance, I'm having a conversation with my Turkish friend and when there is something I don't know how to say in Turkish, I say it in English. The same happens with my Spanish friends from the university, we are having a conversation in Spanish, we then switch to English, or vice versa, or sometimes we are just including random English words in our Spanish conversation.

Finally, I think my interest in language has helped me a lot in life. Even though I haven't yet started a professional career in a field related to what I studied, I have used the languages that I have in my repertoire in a lot of different situations. For instance, when I went to Berlin a couple of years ago, most of the conversations that I had were in Turkish because the big Turkish diaspora that lives there. Also 5 years ago when I went for *the first time to the UK, my taxi driver was Turkish, and I had a great chat with him. I could be talking for hours about how useful English has been in my life. In general, English has helped me to develop myself as a person, learn a lot about the world, travel and, in the future, I hope it will help me to pursuit a career.*

Note how Enrique sometimes uses imaginative language in his narrative. For instance, he writes that he "felt lost" when he first arrived in Spain, but before long he "spoke as a local" and developed a "passion for languages".

- What feelings do you associate with these images?
- Do these metaphoric expressions say something about the importance that Enrique gives to language in his life?

Enrique also writes that he and his brother mix languages to make the "conversation flow smoother" and at several points describes how he integrates different parts of his linguistic repertoire.

- Can you think of other ways to describe this use of language? What metaphors would you use for your own language biography?
- Have you ever heard people mixing languages? Or do you have any personal experiences of translanguaging?

Enrique wrote this narrative after having been presented with the three different tools explored in this guide. His composition follows a linear time-line and illustrates how his language evolved over his lifetime, including critical reflections about the challenges and opportunities that he was given through his linguistic repertoire.

You have just read an autobiographical language narrative (you can find a few more at the end of the book). It is a chronological reflection that tells the writer's life story in relation to language. However, there are many other ways to elicit responses to tell this type of autobiographical narrative. For example, participants can describe a language-related event that happened earlier in their life that they still remember. Or they can answer questions such as the ones below:

Early language exposure

— What was the first language you learned as a child?
— What languages and/or varieties were spoken at home by your family members?
— How did your early environment (e.g. community, school, neighborhood) influence your language learning and use?

Formal education

— What languages were taught at your school?
— Did you receive any formal education in languages other than your native one(s)?

— How did language instruction in school shape your skills and attitudes toward different languages?

Sociocultural influences

— How has your family and cultural background influenced your language use and preferences?
— Have you been part of any communities or social groups that required you to use specific languages or varieties?

Impact of travel and/or migration

— If you have traveled and/or migrated, how did your communicative experience impact your language learning and use?
— What were the challenges and opportunities you encountered in adapting to a new linguistic environment?

Professional impact

— How have language skills influenced your career pursuits?
— Have you had to learn new languages for professional reasons? If so, how did you approach this?

Technological influence

— How has technology (e.g. social media, apps to learn languages, AI-powered translation engines, etc.) influenced your language learning and use?

— Do you use any specific tools or resources to maintain or improve your language skills?

Intergenerational language transmission

— How do you perceive the importance of passing on your language skills to the next generation?

Significant experiences

— Can you describe any memorable experiences related to language learning or use (e.g. traveling, interacting with speakers of other languages)?
— Have you experienced any specific challenges or successes in using different languages or varieties (e.g. times in which the way you speak opened or closed doors for you, or made you feel proud or ashamed)?

Language use and learning

— Which languages/varieties do you use most frequently in your daily life, and in what contexts?
— How do you navigate between different languages in multilingual settings?
— How has learning different languages affected your identity and worldview?
— Are there any languages you wish you had learned or plan to learn in the future? Why?

After having some time to think about these questions, participants can be invited to discuss their answers in pairs or in teams. Once everyone has decided what to write about, they should prepare the next step (the actual narration of their linguistic autobiography). It is important to remind participants of the following:

- Autobiographic accounts do not necessarily have to be linear, nor do they have to start in the past and go up to the present: they can start with our life today, or with our dreams and intentions for the future. It is very common, when recounting our life, to make leaps in time and to select some things and discard others.
- When evaluating events in their life and interpreting what has happened to them, participants should not feel pressure to complete an exhaustive account. On the contrary, the aim is to identify significant landmarks, critical incidents that can be analyzed together when they are shared with others.
- Sometimes it is difficult to put what we have experienced into words. If that is the case, participants should be encouraged to use metaphors, here understood not as a rhetorical device, but as a way of conceptualizing complex concepts in terms of simpler ones, linked to our physical experience. Metaphors are linguistic images that help us to put life into words.
- Usually, when we think of an autobiographical language narrative, we imagine a piece of writing. And rightly so: identifying which facts to tell

and deciding how to present them takes time, and a written format allows participants to organize their thoughts calmly. However, language biographies can also be oral, take the form of a multimodal collage or rest on a timeline that helps visualize someone's life trajectory. They can be freely composed or guided by questions. They can be told on the fly or prepared in advance. Biographies can even be collective (see Workshop proposal). The possibilities are countless. The only requirement is that participants explicitly reflect on the impact of language on their life, and then, ideally, share their language narrative with others to draw some conclusions.

Writing an autobiographic narrative takes time, so it can be set as an assignment to complete at home: see Appendix for a prompt (together with some discussion points that can be projected on a screen as instructions to stimulate debate). And remember: Before composing a story, it is advisable to work in pairs or small teams to identify how to organize the narratives and what elements to include in them.

Once all the narratives have been elaborated, it is also important to share them with the rest of the workshop participants. To do this, each person can take turns reading their work, or a little time can be allotted for participants to select what they want to focus on when telling their story orally. This is feasible if the group is not too large. In a workshop with more than 10 participants, it is probably advisable to divide the group into smaller teams, ask them to share among themselves, then have each team report back to the whole group for a common discussion.

4 Workshop proposal

Safe spaces for conscientization

Before presenting a proposal on how to organize a workshop to address sociolinguistic trajectories, we want to draw attention to the care that accompaniment in sociolinguistic awareness-raising activities requires. Within EquiLing, the search for strategies to mobilize speaker agency and promote a sociolinguistic transformation that challenges power relations and avoids harm led researchers to an important insight. They observed that the experience of language use is not a frequent topic of conversation – not even among those who interact daily and could, therefore, have had the opportunity to talk about it. For this reason, sharing sociolinguistic stories can be intimidating. However, we believe it should be done, because when this conversation happens, and it is handled with care, affect becomes a very powerful drive that can stir a desire for change that envisages a fairer sociolinguistic order.

It is essential to create safe spaces for confidence and trust in which to accompany speakers in their transition to sociolinguistic awareness and agency, so that they dare to share critical linguistic incidents, take on new roles and unleash the power of their languages. Whoever wishes to launch a conscientization space should be aware that, by disclosing events in our history, sometimes traumatic, face-threatening situations can occur. By untying our tongues and all that that encapsulates, unsettling emotions can surface. That is why some caveats are in order, with or without trigger warnings. At all times, whoever conducts the activity must try to foresee issues that may come up, be alert, and try to preserve the emotional well-being of every participant. While encouraging those who feel self-conscious but show they have something to contribute, it is necessary to respect those who want to take refuge in silence.

If first-person testimony seems overwhelming, and participants in a workshop session feel shy or self-conscious talking about themselves, the 'facilitator' leading the workshop can set up dramatization activities in which objects, rather than people, tell stories. This is called object theater and allows, for example, pencils (or anything else acting as a puppet) to verbalize the thoughts and emotions of the participants, providing a detachment that allows greater freedom of expression. Respecting privacy is paramount to avoiding unnecessary risks while deconstructing stereotypes and emphasizing critical insights. Remember that, in the end, the goal is to mobilize critical sociolinguistic awareness and speaker agency, not shun it.

To alleviate any possible emotional burden, participants can also take refuge in the collective. They can, for instance, create communal collages of language experiences, rather than tracing the actual trajectories of individual participants. This is the case of the collage shown on next page, in which participants represent themselves, but not in the first person.

Another way to break the ice is to make a collective linguistic repertoire in the form of a flower. To create this common inventory of the languages

A collectively created collage about language experiences (Santomé, forthcoming)

of those who participate in this task of sociolinguistic reflexivity, colored petal-shaped cards, are needed. First, the colored cards are distributed, and the meaning of each color is explained. In the example provided (see next page), red represents the languages spoken by each participant, so each one, when receiving the red card, must write down which languages and/or varieties they speak. As participants complete the cards, they pass them on to another person and receive a new card of a different color – for example, blue, in which the participants write the languages they are able to understand but not speak. The process continues until everyone has written something on all the cards. With all the petal-shaped cards, a flower is created that represents the collective repertoire of all the participants in the activity. Once the flower is complete, it provides an optimal starting point for discussion and reflection.

red: Languages we speak
blue: Languages we don't speak but understand
green: Languages we can read and understand
purple: Languages we don't speak but have heard
yellow: Languages we don't speak but have seen written
orange: Languages we would like to learn

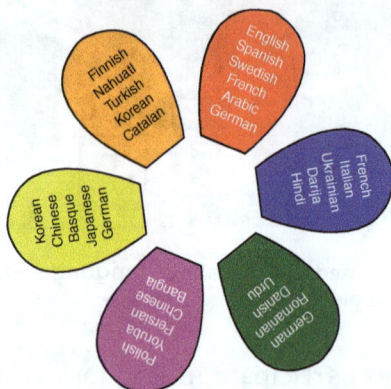

A collective linguistic repertoire in the form of a flower

When people are asked to think about their linguistic repertoire, they are not only asked about the languages they use daily or have a certificate in. They are also asked about the ones they can recognize, even if they don't understand anything; about the ones they would like to learn; about the ones they regret having abandoned. The aim is to identify what the languages of their life mean to them, in the present, in the past or in the future they imagine. Whether it is done in the first person or collectively, when a transformative goal is sought, the most important thing is to reflect and use that reflection as a lever for change. To do this, it is usually recommended to take small steps, therefore following the sequence proposed in this guide can be helpful, as it goes from less to more (both in personal involvement and in degree of detail).

Organizing a workshop

Once the decision to organize a workshop on socio-linguistic trajectories has been made (whether face-to-face or online), the stages proposed below may be of help. These have been designed to explain how to use the tools presented in this guide through an orderly sequence of sessions and activities. Keep in mind that the workshop facilitator does not have to follow the roadmap to the letter, nor do it all. It is possible to choose only one part or modify it to suit the profile of the participants in the activity. The objective (descriptive, not prescriptive) of this chapter is to gather a battery of proposals for facilitators to adapt and make their own, serving as an inspiration bank of activities related to the tools described above. That said, if it is difficult to know how to begin, we suggest the following three stages to support those exploring the languages in their lives. Each one is designed as independent sessions, and can be carried out separately or as follow-up activities on different occasions:

Presentation: An introduction to linguistic biographies and repertoires.

Workshop development: Hands-on work on one, two, or the three tools in the order they are presented in this guide: (i) personal language family trees; (ii) language self-portraits; (iii) autobiographical narratives. We propose this sequence because it progresses from less to more difficult (due to the level of introspection required), but the order can be altered.

Closure: A rounding-up session to elicit proposals to improve the sociolinguistic order identified in the hands-on work session(s).

Thus, if only one of the tools is explored, the workshop will take at least three sessions, but if all three tools are explored, five sessions will be necessary, or even six (if the facilitator decides to include the follow-up activity on language ideologies and language variation and change, described in the next section). However, if more time is available and two sessions are combined into one, fewer days will be needed. In other words, both the number of sessions and their length can be adjusted. As a guideline, the minimum duration we recommend for each session is one hour (60 minutes), with 45 minutes for discussion and 15 minutes for group conclusions. Depending on availability, the discussion can last 1 hour and the brainstorming for conclusions 30 minutes. Or it can all be done in less time, especially if there are few participants. Keep in mind that once the participants feel comfortable and relaxed, they usually have a lot to share, so it is not advisable to allow less time than indicated. Remember also that the time factor is important so as not to force anyone to rush their confidences. And remember that personal experiences will be shared, so a warm-up could be necessary.

The table below contains a proposal for the entire workshop. In the Appendix there are ready-to-use materials that can be of help to dynamize the sessions or to set preparatory work.

OVERVIEW OF THE WORKSHOP

Session	Description of sessions and activities
PRESENTATION What will we do? One person, the facilitator, leads the workshop. All sessions and activities can be carried out online/ offline.	A 60-minute session in which the facilitator presents the topic of the entire workshop, the activities to be done in different sessions and why it is important to reflect on the languages we live by: (i) exploring languages in the family of participants and creating personal language trees, (ii) drawing language self-portraits, (iii) recounting autobiographical language narratives.

The next step is a review of sociolinguistic concepts. The facilitator should make sure that relevant concepts are known by participants. The explanatory texts in this guide and the glossary can be of help at this point. However, it is important not to overwhelm the participants by presenting too many concepts at the beginning: there will also be opportunities to deepen the concepts during the different sessions.

If working collectively, the working teams are organized. Since many of the activities (especially before the hands-on sessions) are individual, an important part of the workshop is sharing experiences in small groups, seeing other points of view, approaching unknown aspects of people and commenting on linguistic experiences as a group.

If the facilitator wants to start the next session with something that the participants must bring from home (for instance, a family tree), it should be announced now.

The first session serves to introduce participants to concepts that can open their eyes to critical sociolinguistic awareness, so that later on in the workshop they can identify life milestones marked by language and critically analyze the impact of languages on their lives. Depending on their age, background, and previous theoretical knowledge, adjustments will have to be made. In any event, and to ensure that everyone has the necessary background, a brief introduction to the following concepts may be useful: linguistic biographies, linguistic repertoires, linguistic socialization, and life trajectories. In addition to the explanations throughout the guide, further readings are listed in Chapter 5: To learn more.

After presenting the fundamental concepts, and as a warm-up activity, participants can be asked to share moments in their socialization when they felt they were being surveilled because of the way they spoke, because they were told how (not) to speak, or because they were mocked or criticized for speaking in a certain way. It is important for the workshop facilitator to disclose personal experiences, so that the rest of the participants can eventually dare to tell their own. In the next step, all of them can then be compared and discussed.

Ultimately, it is all about drawing attention to sociolinguistic injustice and stimulating critical awareness, so it is necessary to allow time for participants to share their experiences. Remember that those who do not usually verbalize their sociolinguistic trajectories may need more time and support.

WORKSHOP (I)
Personal language family trees

The facilitator leads the session. Ideally, the participants gather information from their families in advance and bring their drawings of family trees to class. Failing that, they draw their trees on the spot and the discussion time is shortened.

A 60-minute session, with 45 minutes for discussion and 15 minutes to reach conclusions as a group.

During the discussion time, participants describe their language family trees in pairs or small teams. Afterwards, the group discusses striking facts raised during the individual accounts.

If the facilitator wants to start the next session with something that the participants must bring from home (for instance, a language self-portrait), it should be announced now.

WORKSHOP (II)
Language self-portraits

The facilitator leads the session. Ideally, the participants have identified in advance the main components to be drawn in their language portraits. Failing that, they do so at the beginning of the session, and the drawing and discussion time is shortened.

A 60-minute session, with 45 minutes for discussion and 15 minutes to reach conclusions as a group.

During the discussion time, participants draw and describe their language portraits, then the group discusses striking facts raised during the individual accounts.

If the facilitator wants to start the next session with something that the participants must bring from home (e.g. the autobiographical language narrative), it should be announced now.

WORKSHOP (III)
Autobiographical language narratives

The facilitator leads the session. Ideally, the participants have written their autobiographies in advance (in full or at least identifying significant turning points). Failing that, they do so at the beginning of the session and the discussion time is shortened.

A 60-minute session, with 45 minutes for discussion and 15 minutes to reach conclusions as a group.

During the discussion time, participants tell their language narratives, then the group discusses striking facts raised during the individual accounts. The following questions may fuel the debate:

- What did you learn in this workshop about language narratives?
- Was there anything that you found surprising?
- How did you feel while telling your story and listening to others?

If the facilitator wants to start the next session with something that the participants must bring from home (e.g. reflections on changes in their repertoire over time, marked patterns of variation, or proposals for transforming the socio-linguistic situation discovered while exploring the tools in this book), it should be announced now.

WORKSHOP (IV)
Follow-up activity: Language variation and change, language ideologies, and AI

A 60-minute session, with 45 minutes for discussion and 15 minutes to reach conclusions as a group.

The facilitator leads the session. Ideally, the participants have identified moments of change in their repertoire or environments/situations in which they have experienced a clear pattern of variation (e.g. when vacationing elsewhere, communicating online, or using AI tools). Failing that, they do so at the beginning of the session and the discussion time is shortened.

During the discussion time, participants draw and/or describe changes in their linguistic repertoire over time and/or patterns of linguistic variation that, in deviating from the norm, trigger ideological reactions. The group then discusses striking facts raised during the individual accounts.

If the facilitator wants to start the next session with something that the participants must bring from home (e.g. proposals to improve and transform the existing situation), it should be announced now.

CLOSURE (V)
What can we do to make it better?

A 60-minute session, with 45 minutes to discuss proposals in pairs or teams (participants can fill out the transformational proposals sheet below to systematize their ideas and make the proposals more operative) and 15 minutes to reach conclusions as a group.

The facilitator leads the session, encouraging the systematization of collective transformative proposals (arising from the discussion in previous sessions) on how to develop a more sustainable and just sociolinguistic environment.

Ideally, after the session, the participants create something (e.g. a short video, a post on social media, an infographic, a poster) to make their findings known.

If time permits it, all participants can showcase their drawings of family trees and linguistic self-portraits in the form of an 'art exhibition'.

TRANSFORMATIONAL PROPOSALS SHEET

Statement of the proposal	What collective action will we put in place to improve the reality we have analyzed?
What the proposal addresses	What specific problem do we believe this action helps to solve?
Objectives	What are the specific objectives of this action?
When and where	At what specific time and place can we do this?
Who	What people, organizations or institutions can we involve in putting the plan into practice?
Tools	What kind of tools can we use (artistic, linguistic, technological, communicative or political)?
Steps	How can we carry out this action step by step? How can we do this to not only state ideals, but to create a realistic plan?
Schedule	On what dates will each step take place and who will be in charge of each necessary step?
Ethical considerations	What are the ethical risks of this proposal? What measures can be taken to ensure that the action will respect the rights of participants or spectators?

Follow-up activity: language variation and change, language ideologies, and reflection on AI

If workshop participants are interested in digging deeper into theoretical and abstract sociolinguistic concepts, this optional follow-up activity can be undertaken after the workshop. It can also be done before the closure session.

Throughout this guide, we have often underlined that our linguistic repertoires are never static but change over time as our lives change. We have also emphasized that the attitudes of others (and socially prevailing language ideologies) play a crucial role in how we perceive ourselves and how others perceive us. Consequently, these beliefs and attitudes affect our linguistic habits and choices.

Look, for example, at the way Taamasi, a young Indian girl, represents the transition between her different languages when she distinguishes her linguistic profile before and after her twenties. In the first case, she chose to draw circles to focus on the points of contact between the languages in her life, rather than placing each language somewhere on her portrait to reflect the significance of each language.

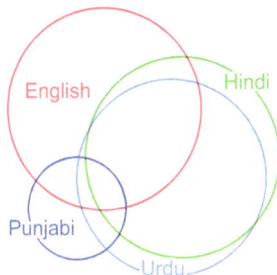

Repertoire ages 0-20: Core languages

Taamasi's repertoire before her twenties

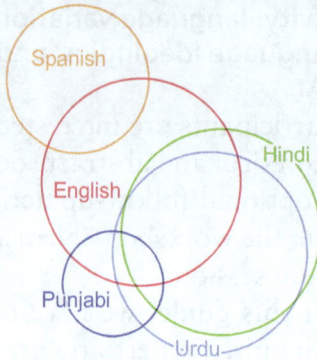

Repertoire ages 20-23: Spanish became a part of my repertoire, but I didn't consider it as a 'core language'. I thought of Spanish as a separate category – sometimes mixing it with English

Taamasi's repertoire after the age of twenty

Notice how, at one point, a new language, Spanish, entered her repertoire and how she connects Spanish with English.

- Why do you think the new addition is linked to English, but not to her other languages?
- In your case, how would you display the languages you are learning, but have not yet mastered?
- And what about the languages you once learned but no longer use?

Instead of drawing your repertoire at a single point in time (such as Taamasi's repertoire in the figure above), you can also do it over time. Such a diachronic portrait will tell you a lot about what has been happening to you throughout your life. If, on the other hand, you do not chart modifications in your repertoire diachronically but depending on the context, then you will not be paying attention to change, but to variation. This is what Taamasi does in the following circles, in which she breaks down all the different ways in which she uses English, rather than sticking to a single label.

If you think about it, this breakdown of languages has significant implications:

- Why does Taamasi use Hinglish (a blend of the words Hindi and English) with people in her close circle and standard English for study and work?
- Do you think this difference between the languages she uses in different contexts is a personal choice or is it imposed?
- How many varieties of English do you know? Which one(s) do you use, in what context and why?

It makes no sense to speak of English (or any other language) as if it were a single monolithic entity, because it is an umbrella term that encompasses many different realities. However, it is interesting to observe how we talk about different variants of English.

- Have you ever heard of the term 'Englishes'?
- How could you break down the language you consider your main language into parts? Feel free to include not only varieties but also registers, accents, and explain what you associate each of them with.

I'd like to further divide the English
I use into the following categories

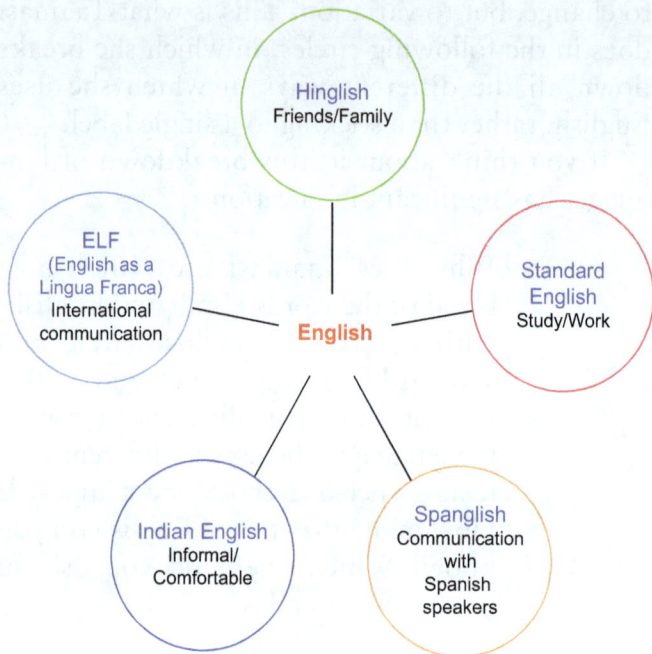

The different 'Englishes' in Taamasi's life

Let us now stop for a moment and think about
Spanglish, which Taamasi mentions as well.

- At what point does one language (be it
  Spanish, English or any other) stop
  being that language and start being
  something else? Does it matter?
- If you answered yes, then you probably
  think it is a shame that Latin became
  Spanish, French, Romanian etc. Or
  maybe not? Why?

Language variation and change always confront us with our language ideologies. Often, those beliefs have a deep impact on our everyday lives, even if we rarely notice them. We invite you to try and note not only how you speak, but also how you think about language.

For starters, think of all the times you have heard complaints about how young people talk. Do not think this complaint is something new, it has been going on for as long as the world has existed. But it does not mean the language is getting worse and worse, or that new generations are more ignorant. It just means human beings often reject uncertainty, the unknown, and so become fearful of change. However, if there is one thing that is constantly changing, it is language. Language is changing all the time, non-stop, because it has to respond to the needs of the speakers, which are also very changeable.

Whenever we come in contact and communicate with others, even if we do not realize it, we change. This is also true of language, which inevitably changes over time. In fact, the only languages that do not change are dead languages, which no longer have speakers to make them evolve. But beware! 'Evolve' does not mean 'get better' or 'get worse': it simply means to change, to become something different. However, for whatever reason, we are almost always afraid of difference, so we often reject change without realizing that, whether we reject it or not, it is going to happen.

Think about yourself and answer these three questions:

- Do you speak exactly the same way you did when you were much younger?
- Do you speak exactly the same way with everyone (including yourself)?
- Do you speak exactly the same way in different social situations?

The answer, for sure, will be a resounding 'no' in every case. This is called linguistic variation, and it is something that all human beings have in common. It is also, ultimately, the reason why there are different varieties of all the languages of the world. Sometimes the varieties are so different from one another that we end up giving them a different name. We say that they are two different languages. But no matter how we categorize them, for individual speakers, they are part of a single whole within us: our linguistic repertoire.

It is also interesting to reflect on variation, change and linguistic ideologies in relation to the new technical linguistic supports of AI (artificial intelligence):

- What will happen with our languages when we use machines to think, write and correct our texts?
- What kind of texts are used to inform AI programs? Who has written them? Do these texts reflect different language varieties?
- What about the spoken language used to inform AI programs? Are all languages equally represented in them?

- What consequences will AI have for translation between languages?
- Are there any foreseeable consequences for languages with fewer speakers? And what about a world language such as English?

Researchers who have explored AI programs have noticed that producing 'multilingual creativity' is not a real possibility, not yet at least. It is still too early to know how these programs will impact our language learning, use and creativity in the future. But preliminary findings indicate that people who use AI tools in their writing (be it emails, school texts or personal letters) will increasingly reinforce normative standard variants, rather than diversity. Perhaps this is something that, after having analyzed our repertoires and how they intermingle with our lives, we should think about. For instance, it is still impossible for an AI program to create your language portrait or your autobiographical language narrative without providing a lot of personal information beforehand.

Expected outcomes from using this guide

This guide, a spin-off of the EquiLing research project, presents tools for exploring linguistic biographies and repertoires, as well as a workshop proposal for their implementation. The goal is to invite critical reflection on language, power relations and identities – not only at the individual level, but also in society. In our experience, this line of work can help accomplish valuable outcomes, such as:

Safe spaces for linguistic reflection and conscientization: The creation of safe spaces is both a prerequisite and a result of the activities proposed in this volume. When participants learn to reflect on their sociolinguistic trajectories and apply theoretical concepts to their experiences, they can modify the way they think and feel about linguistic practices and ideologies and move towards language-related conscientization. To our mind, this newly gained critical awareness fosters a sense of resilience and promotes agency. But for this to happen, it is vital that participants dare to engage in a dialogical environment without fearing judgement.

Reflexivity through critical incidents: Reflecting on life experiences in which language practices have been met with negative reactions, sometimes even marginalization, helps us understand the impact of language in the articulation of inequality. Such reflexivity can, in turn, lead to a better understanding of language ideologies and the socio-political structures influencing people's trajectories. The sharing of critical incidents can also create empathy and solidarity among participants, especially when they realize that what may have seemed like an isolated personal experience is a part of broader social patterns.

Confidence and legitimacy: Through narrative sharing in structured workshops, participants can begin to dismantle normative judgments that cast their linguistic practices as inferior or 'illegitimate'. By reinterpreting their practices and identities, participants can gain confidence and start embracing their linguistic repertoires as valuable resources. They can also start contesting feelings of shame or inadequacy and replace negative emotions with more constructive feelings.

Socially informed language practices: In our experience, when participants share, question and reframe their language practices together, they start to question, challenge and resist linguistic inequalities. Consequently, they also start to envision a more just linguistic environment by proposing socially informed language practices that can lead to both personal and social transformation.

For all these reasons, we invite you on a journey to explore linguistic biographies and linguistic repertoires that helps put curiosity and critical reflexivity about language in service of social justice.

5 To learn more

Glossary

The terms in the glossary systematize sociolinguistic concepts and processes addressed throughout this guide. It can be consulted by the workshop facilitator and the participants before, during and after the activities. As in all cases, it is recommended to encourage participants to share doubts about these terms, because they not only help clarify concepts but also help to bring to light experiences that can be analyzed as a team.

Agency: The ability to act and direct our lives, instead of behaving as passive subjects to whom things happen. It is the opposite of helplessness, and, in the case of speaker agency, it has to do with their empowerment in the face of discriminatory ideologies and practices that demean people because of the way they speak.

Critical language awareness: The act of realizing how language, privilege and power relate to each other and how this influences our identities and our practices as speakers. The first step to gaining such awareness is to note that language is situated in a social context that marks many aspects of language that go beyond language itself.

Critical linguistic incidents: Situations in our lives in which our way of speaking had a negative impact on us, and that remain etched in our minds because of the strong emotions they evoked. Verbalizing such critical incidents can not only trigger self-understanding, but also empathy from others, and sometimes even a collective desire for change.

Conscientization: A pedagogical approach inspired by Paulo Freire that helps to (i) increase the capacity to reflect about language in general, and the languages of individuals and communities; (ii) understand the causes that explain one's own linguistic experiences; and (iii) foster the will to transform how languages are valued and organized in a community.

Language ideologies: A set of beliefs, which are part of the common sense of a community, about languages, speech and/or communication, and that are linked to specific political and sociocultural realities. They have, therefore, repercussions on the *status quo*, naturalizing and normalizing it. These ideologies, moreover, explain how we use language daily, which is why they persist over time.

Linguistic diversity: The result of the coexistence of different languages in the same territory or speech community. Although it sometimes involves conflicts, it is an extraordinarily rich situation (culturally, linguistically and socially) and advocates respect for all languages, promoting the preservation of those that are at risk due to lack of speakers, or lack of contexts to use them.

Linguistic citizenship: This concept addresses who should be recognized as a legitimate speaker within a community and whether adherence to a standardized language or a historically established national variety is mandatory to achieve this status. Understanding language through the lens of citizenship also invites us to rethink our understanding of citizenship through the lens of language. This concept is gaining salience in sociolinguistic research, since it construes language as a site of political struggle and frames it as an important tool for obtaining agency, transformation and parity of participation through the use of language (registers, etc.) in circumstances that may be embedded in, or outside of, institutionalized democratic frameworks.

Linguistic marginalization: Treating people as if they were not important because of the languages and/or varieties they speak, or do not speak. This results in a lack of recognition, and limits their access to opportunities or to participation in society.

Linguistic socialization: The process whereby people, through social interaction, acquire one or more languages and develop communicative skills. It has to do with how, where, with whom, and for what purposes we learn and acquire language as individuals, whether it is our first language(s) or others acquired later in life.

Speakerhood: This term relates to the social construction of what it means to be a 'good speaker' of a language. A 'native speaker' model is often imposed on language learners, which is based on a rather vague idea of competence that is often unattainable for those learning a language as adults. The various imposed models of speakerhood (such as the 'native speaker', the 'neutral speaker', or the 'migrant speaker') function as mechanisms of subjectification and governance and risk generating subaltern speaker subjectivities that generate feelings of shame, inferiority and insecurity.

More concepts and definitions are included in the EquiLing open-access guide *Street languages: Collective landscapes of the languages that surround us. A guide to promote critical sociolinguistic awareness*, available for download in English: https://octaedro.com/libro/street-languages-collective-landscapes-of-the-languages-that-surround-us/ and in Spanish: https://octaedro.com/libro/lenguas-callejeras-paisajes-colectivos-de-las-lenguas-que-nos-rodean/

A glossary with other definitions are available on the EquiLing website: https://www.equiling.eu/en/blog/glossary/

References

The following is a concise list of books and articles produced by the EquiLing team, as well as a selection of references in the domain of critical sociolinguistic awareness or linguistic biographies and repertoires. These readings may be useful to delve deeper into the concepts, activities and tools proposed in this guide, and to learn more about how to apply similar tools in different contexts.

Academic publications from EquiLing

Martín Rojo, L., Pujolar, J. and Amorrortu, E. (eds) (2025) *Negotiating Sociolinguistic Justice: Turning Spaces of Inequality into Spaces of Conscientization*. Special issue of *International Journal of the Sociology of Language*: Available at https://www.degruyterbrill.com/journal/key/ijsl/2025/291/html?srsltid=AfmBOor7D6hz8AIPvdzBt7XvV5b_2mlkUREfDsE-KlJRGpYBiW0jBqpO
This special issue contains several articles on theoretical issues related to the unequal distribution of linguistic resources, the unequal recognition of speakers, and parity of participation (addressing topics such as linguistic surveillance, speaker agency, or conscientization spaces).

Goirigolzarri Garaizar, J. and Alonso, L. (eds) (2025) *In Search of Sociolinguistic Justice: Mobilizing Transformative Agency through Action-research*. Special issue of Language Policy Journal. Available at https://link.springer.com/collections/gfbiffbeic
This special issue contains several articles on methodological issues addressed within the project (such as the role of researchers in Participatory Action Research or the creation of epistemic communities).

Prego Vázquez, G., Caamaño Rojo, M. and Zas Varela, L. (2025) Ideoloxías lingüísticas na representación da diversidades na aula. In E. Fernández Rey, M. Guisantes

Alonso and E. Fidalgo Garra (eds) *Identidades e ideo-loxías lingüísticas perante a diversidade lingüística.* Consello da Cultura Galega.

This article explains how object theater can be used to raise critical language awareness.

Santomé, V. (forthcoming) *Non hai fronteiras: comuni-dades para la reflexión sociolingüística crítica mediante biografías lingüísticas colectivas en contextos de minorización. PhD dissertation.* Universidad Autónoma de Madrid.

This doctoral thesis addresses the creation of collective collages in depth.

Bank of resources to enhance critical sociolinguistic awareness

This is a list of similar projects available online at the time of launching this guide. Over time, some links may break and no longer be retrievable.

Arts and Humanities Research Council (2021) *We are Multilingual.* Available at https://www.wamcam.org/

Beacco, J.-C., Byram, M., Cavalli, M., Coste, D., Egli Cuenat, M., Goullier, F. and Panthier, J. (2016) *Guide for the Development and Implementation of Curricula for Plurilingual and Intercultural Education.* Available at https://www.coe.int/en/web/language-policy/guide-for-the-development-and-implementation-of-curricula-for-plurilingual-and-intercultural-education

Calamai, S. (2022) *The Circe Project: Counteracting Accent Discrimination Practices in Education.* Available at https://www.circe-project.eu/

Casa Asia (2021) *Autobiografías lingüísticas: ¿somos lo que hablamos?* Available at https://www.casaasia.es/actuali-dad/autobiografias-linguisticas-somos-lo-que-hablamos/

Council of Europe (2001) *The Language Biography.* Available at https://www.coe.int/en/web/portfolio/the-language-biography

Council of Europe (2006) *The Autobiography of Intercultural Encounters*. Available at https://www.coe.int/en/web/autobiography-intercultural-encounters/home

Drummond, R. and Amanda, C. (2019) *The accentism project*. Available at https://accentism.org/

Galante, A. (2017) *Breaking the Invisible Wall*. Available at https://www.breakingtheinvisiblewall.com/

Galante, A., Chiras, M., de la Cruz J.W.N. and Zeaiter, L.F. (2022) *Plurilingual Guide: Implementing Critical Plurilingual Pedagogy in Language Education*. Plurilingual Lab Publishing. Available at https://www.mcgill.ca/plurilinguallab/files/plurilinguallab/plurilingual%20_guide.pdf

Gray, J. (2021) *Recognising and Including LGBTQ+ Identities in Language Teaching*. Available at https://www.ucl.ac.uk/teaching-learning/publications/2021/jun/recognising-and-including-lgbtq-identities-language-teaching

Hanover Research (2019) Cultural awareness and cultural competence toolkit. Available at https://cpb-us-e1.wpmucdn.com/blogs.gwu.edu/dist/a/3589/files/2021/03/Cultural-Awareness-and-Competence-Toolkit.pdf

Institut national des langues et civilisations orientales (2024) *'Ma vie, ma langue', an original RFI podcast in partnership with Inalco University*. Available at https://www.inalco.fr/en/news/ma-vie-ma-langue-original-rfi-podcast-partnership-inalco-university

Khol, K. (2016) *Creative Multilingualism*. Available at https://www.creativeml.ox.ac.uk/

Kiczkowiak, M. (2017) Confronting native speakerism in the ELT classroom: Practical awareness-raising activities. *The European Journal of Applied Linguistics and TEFL* 6/1. Available at https://www.researchgate.net/publication/317545428_CONFRONTING_NATIVE_SPEAKERISM_IN_THE_ELT_CLASSROOM_PRACTICAL_AWARENESS-RAISING_ACTIVITIES

León-Howarth, K. and Mendoza C.H. (2021) *A Short Introduction to Basic Concepts of Sociolinguistics, and the Role of Prescriptive Organizations Like the Real Academia Española*. Open Education Resource. Available at https://human.libretexts.org/Bookshelves/Languages/Spanish/Empowering_Learners_of_Spanish/01%3A_Unidades_(Lessons)/1.01%3A_Introductory_Lesson-_An_overview_of_sociolinguistics

Luppi, R. and Eva-Maria, T. (2022) *Biografie linguistiche. Esempi di linguistica applicata*. Quaderni del CeSLiC Occasional Papers. Available at https://amsacta.unibo.it/id/eprint/6849/

Multilingual Families Project. Activities to support multilingualism at school. Available at https://www.skolapelican.com/wp-content/uploads/2015/05/Activities-to-support-multilingualism-at-school.pdf

Open University, The (2017) Multilingualism in the classroom. Available at https://docslib.org/doc/9474150/multilingualism-in-the-classroom-tess-india-resource

Otheguy, R., García, O. and Menken, K. (2021) CUNY-NYSIEB *Initiative for Emergent Bilinguals*. Available at www.cuny-nysieb.org

Piller, I. (2011) *Language on the Move*. Available at https://www.languageonthemove.com/ingrid-piller/

Scoilnet (2025) Cultural and linguistic supports. Available at https://www.scoilnet.ie/go-to-primary/clsupports/

Social Sciences and Humanities Research Council of Canada (2019) *Me Mapping with Multilingual Learners*. Available at https://sites.google.com/view/memapping/home

Volkmer, A. (2018) *Language Justice Curriculum*. Center for Participatory Change. Available at https://static1.squarespace.com/static/65a6df5e577ee4447ca9ea1a/t/6627d33b0c72ae267e637d6c/1713886016732/CPC+-+Language+Justice+Curriculum+May+2018.pdf

Other relevant academic publications

Ahlgren, K. (2019) Art as a trigger for reflection in sociolinguistic migration research. *Journal of Mediterranean Knowledge-JMK* 4 (2), 203–222, Special Issue: Artistic

Strategies of Migration: Art as a Resistance or as a Reinsurance?

Ahlgren, K. (2021) Poetic representations: A process of writing nearby. *Journal of Sociolinguistics* 5, 832–851.

Blommaert, J. and Backus, Ad. (2013) Superdiverse repertoires and the individual. In I. de Saint-Georges and J.J. Weber (eds) *Multilingualism and Multimodality: The Future of Education Research* (pp. 11–32). Sense Publishers.

Busch, B., Aziza, J. and Angelika, T. (2006) *Language Biographies for Multilingual Learning.* PRAESA.

Busch, B. and McNamara, T. (2020) Language and trauma. *Applied Linguistics* 41 (3), 323–333.

Coste, D. (2022) Some elements of family history and language biography. In G. Prasad, N. Auger and E. Le Pichon Vorstman (eds) *Multilingualism and Education: Researchers' Pathways and Perspectives* (pp. 92–103). Cambridge University Press.

Council of Europe (2020) *Common European Framework of Reference for Languages: Learning, Teaching, Assessment.* Companion volume. Strasbourg: Council of Europe.

Crookes, G.V. (2022) Critical language pedagogy. *Language Teaching* 55, 46–63.

Cummins, J., Ntelioglou, B.Y., Prasad, G. and Stille, S. (2017) Identity text projects. In J.B. Cummings and M.L. Blatherwick (eds) *Creative Dimensions of Teaching and Learning in the 21st Century: Advances in Creativity and Giftedness.* Sense Publishers.

Dragojevic, M., Fasoli, F., Cramer, J. and Rakić, T. (2021) Toward a century of language attitudes research: Looking back and moving forward. *Journal of Language and Social Psychology* 40 (1), 60–79.

Franceschini, R. (2022) Language biographies. *Sociolinguistica* 36 (1–2), 69–83.

Freire, P. (1970) *Pedagogy of the Oppressed.* Continuum.

Freire, P. (1993) *Política e educação.* Cortez.

Freire, P. (2014) *Pedagogy of Hope.* Bloomsbury Academic.

Galante, A. (2025) Plurilingual and pluricultural competence: Origins, current trends, and future directions. In C. Fäcke, A. Gao and P. Garrett-Rucks (eds) *The Handbook of Plurilingual and Intercultural Language Learning* (pp. 333–348). Wiley.

García, O. (2008) Multilingual language awareness and teacher education. In J. Cenoz and N. Hornberger (eds) *Encyclopedia of Language and Education* (pp. 385–400). Springer.

García, O. (2016) Critical multilingual language awareness and teacher education. In J. Cenoz, D. Gorter and S. May (eds) *Language Awareness and Multilingualism* (pp. 1–17). Springer.

Holguín Mendoza, C. (2022) Sociolinguistic justice and student agency in language education: Towards a model for critical sociocultural linguistics literacy. In S. Loza and S Beaudrie (eds) *Teaching Languages Critically* (pp. 138–156). Routledge.

Kusters, A. and M. De Meulder, M. (2019) Language portraits: Investigating embodied multilingual and multimodal repertoires. *Forum Qualitative Sozialforschung* 20 (3), 10.

Lakoff, G. and Johnsson, M. (1980) *Metaphors We Live By.* University of Chicago Press.

Mendelowitz, B., Ferreira, A. and Kerryn Dixon, A. (2022) *Language Narratives and Shifting Multilingual Pedagogies: English Teaching from the South.* Bloomsbury.

Miyahara, M. (2015) *Emerging Self-Identities and Emotion in Foreign Language Learning: A Narrative-Oriented Approach.* Multilingual Matters.

Molina, C. (2024) Shame on me: The individual whitewash of a social stigma underpinned by language ideologies. *Multilingua* 43 (1), 35–62.

Nunan, D. and J. Choi, J. (eds) (2010) *Language and Culture: Reflective Narratives and the Emergence of Identity.* Routledge.

Piller, I., Butorac, D., Farrell, E., Lising, L., Motaghi-Tabari, S. and Tetteh, V.W. (2024) *Life in a New Language.* Oxford University Press.

Purkarthofer, J. and Flubacher M.-C. (eds) (2022) *Speaking Subjects in Multilingualism Research: Biographical and Speaker-centred Approaches*. Multilingual Matters.

Rose, H. and Nicola Galloway, N. (2017) Debating standard language ideology in the classroom: Using the 'Speak Good English Movement' to raise awareness of global Englishes. *RELC Journal* 48 (3), 294–301.

Stroud, C. and Kerfoot C. (2021) Decolonizing higher education. Multilingualism, linguistic citizenship and epistemic justice. In Z. Bock and C. Stroud (eds) *Reclaiming Voice: Language and Decoloniality in Higher Education* (pp. 21–51). Bloomsbury.

Tissari, H. (2022) Expressions of emotion and linguistic change. In G.L. Schiewer, J. Altarriba and N.B. Chin (eds) *Language and Emotion: An International Handbook* (pp. 302–323). Mouton de Gruyter.

Woolard, K. (2021) Language ideology. In J. Stanlaw (ed.) *The International Encyclopedia of Linguistic Anthropology* (pp. 1–21). Wiley.

Appendix: Ready-to-use materials

The following materials can be adapted by facilitators to match the needs of workshop participants.

Questions to encourage discussion in the workshop sessions

Make an inventory of your linguistic repertoire, and explain in what contexts you activate your different linguistic resources:

- What do these languages, dialects, varieties and accents reveal about our life and background? And about our society?
- Are these languages, dialects, varieties and accents represented in the linguistic landscape of your neighborhood, that is, signage on public space, in public transportation or in the place where you study/work? In restaurants and shops?
- Are these languages, dialects, varieties and accents part of the everyday life of your community? Or are they something you only share with the members of your household?

Reflect individually over the following questions:

- Have you ever tried to change the way you speak? If so, what did you try to avoid and/or what did you imitate from others? Why?
- Have you experienced prejudice because of the way you speak? What did you do if that was the case and how did you feel about it?
- Do you think that there are any dialects, varieties and accents that influence your personal image?
- Are you studying any languages? Did you in the past? Why did you choose that/those language(s)? What or who influenced your decision? What do the people around you think about you studying that/those language(s)?

Discuss together with others:

- What does a person's linguistic repertoire reflect about their life trajectory?
- What makes a person's linguistic repertoire change over time?
- What is the impact of language policies and ideologies on individual and collective linguistic repertoires?
- Why are there more and more hybrid linguistic practices in contemporary societies?

Prompts for exploring the three tools

Using 'unexpected' language varieties, having an accent (we all have one) or mixing languages is often a source of prejudice. To avoid reproach or discrimination, a lot of people try to alter the way they speak. However, language-related biases are often naturalized, so we need critical language awareness to face them. One way to raise awareness is by exploring our linguistic repertoires and biographies. We will do it in three steps:

(i) **Personal language family tree**

Sketch a family tree in which you record all the languages, dialects and/or varieties spoken in your family (perhaps you, your parents and grandparents is enough). You do not need to follow any model for the drawing, but you should ask yourself (and your relatives) a series of questions before you sketch your own tree:

- What languages do you speak? What varieties and dialects?
- How many languages can you recognize even if you do not know them?
- Is there any language you can read but not speak? Or the other way round?
- Is there any language that you used to speak but have forgotten? How did that happen? Do you regret it, or do you really not care?

- Is there any language you wish your parents had taught you? Why didn't they?
- At school, why did you learn English (or whatever language you learned) instead of another language? Did you choose for yourself or did your family or school decide for you? Are you happy with this choice? Why? Why not?

Once you have traced your own language family tree, interviews with relatives can help to understand some of the whys and wherefores:

- Why do your relatives speak (whatever language/variety) at home instead of any other?
- Are there any languages they were forced to learn, or forbidden to speak, at some point?
- How do they feel about the different languages in their repertoires? How do these repertoires reflect their life choices?

There are so many questions you can ask yourself and others about languages in the family! Can you expand the list with additional questions?

(ii) Language self-portrait

Draw a language portrait of yourself to describe your language repertoire (the languages, dialects, varieties and accents within you). You don't need to follow any models for the drawing, but you should think about the answer to these questions to get started:

- What language(s), varieties and dialects do you use in your daily interactions?
- Where would you place them in your body?
- What color will you use for each language?
- Do you speak, write or understand any other dialect or variety that do not have an 'official name'?
- Are there any languages you are learning, but have not yet mastered? Any languages you want to learn in the future? How could you represent all those in the portrait?

(iii) Autobiographical language narrative

Write your own language narrative. Before writing, you should take some time to reflect on your linguistic repertoire and the role that languages play in your life:

- When and with whom do you use each language, dialect, variety and accent?
- Why do you use those languages and varieties in those contexts but not in others?
- What significant language-related landmarks have you experienced at different times and places in your life?
- Which language(s) have you learnt, and which one would you like to learn? Why?
- Is there any language(s) someone wants you to learn/use, but you do not? And what do you feel about that?
- What are the languages you used to know, but have now forgotten? Why?
- Are there any opportunities that languages have granted or denied you?

You can also discuss what the languages in your repertoire reveal about you and your life trajectory, and how and why your view of languages and identity has changed over time. Or you can discuss a critical incident you have experienced as a language user/learner, that is, your memories of a significant negative or positive event. Describe also how you reacted to what happened, what you think it says about you, and whether you have changed ever since.

You do not have to follow any specific format or a chronological order to complete this task, but we recommend that your narrative is no longer than 1000 words (no more than 2 pages). Write in the first person, include any drawings or graphics you wish, and feel free to include personal anecdotes. Most importantly, reflect on how your identity is related (i) to the linguistic practices you have identified within your repertoire and (ii) to your experiences with the language at different places and times in your life.

Prompt to set an autobiographical language narrative as homework before the workshop.

- Reflect on the languages, varieties and linguistic practices that are, have been or you want to be part of your linguistic repertoire and how they relate to your identity. To do that, think about language-related experiences (by 'language' you can also refer to dialects, varieties or accents) that you have, or have had, at different times or places. Think, also, about the reasons why you want to learn some languages rather than others, the doors that languages have opened or closed for you and so on.
- Write your linguistic autobiography (maximum 1,000 words) explaining where, when,

in what context, and with whom you speak each of the languages, dialects, varieties or accents in your repertoire. You can also write about the languages you would like to learn (and why), the languages you used to know but have forgotten (and why), or the languages you don't speak but are able to recognize.

- Write in the first person, do not hesitate to include personal anecdotes, and try to relate your experiences to whatever you learned throughout the workshop. You do not need to follow any model, just reflect on your linguistic practices and on how your identity has changed after analyzing the role that languages play in our life trajectory.

- If you want, you can include drawings or diagrams to show your repertoire, your family's repertoire, or that of people who play an important role in your life.

Autobiographical narratives for inspiration

In the following pages you will find autobiographical narratives written by multilingual university students taking a course in sociolinguistics as part of a master's degree in applied linguistics in Spain. The texts display the richness of the reflections that come from focusing on their sociolinguistic trajectories and from discussions with other students during workshops.

Yildiz (a young woman born in Turkey)

It is amazing how knowing/speaking/understanding languages shapes all our perspectives in life. I have always been amazed by the power of language, and I believe my interest was aroused because of the different backgrounds and languages I was exposed to in childhood. I was born into a partially Arabic-speaking Turkish family where my mum did not speak Arabic until she was in her early twenties. She was exposed to her parents speaking Arabic, but she didn't want to speak it because Arabic was considered a language spoken by the villagers or farmers. So, my mother or father never spoke to me in Arabic, but I heard and listened to it from my grandparents all the time.

One summer, when I was 5 years old, I spent 6 months with my paternal grandparents. While I stayed in Syria, my mother and I were intensely exposed to the Syrian dialect of Arabic, and when I came back to Turkey to start kindergarten, I had forgotten how to speak Turkish. As I was immersed in the school environment, I was able to pick up Turkish fast and went back to speaking my mother tongue. After that, we had to move to Saudi Arabia due to my father's job and my parents decided to move me into a school where the language of instruction was only English. Both the students and the teachers were mainly Sri Lankans, Bangladeshis, Indians, and Pakistanis. Then, two years later, I had to change to a school with English Medium Instruction with Bangladeshi teachers, yet with students of many nationalities, from the Philippines, Iraq, Russia, Lebanon and Egypt, in addition to the nationalities mentioned above. Having studied in this school for two years, I had to change my school again to a place where some of my teachers were Canadian, British, Lebanese, and with students from different nationalities in addition to the ones above. This included Americans, British, Mexican, Russian, Jordanian-American, and Lebanese-American. My best friend at that time was a girl who was from Bangladesh who spoke with an American accent and therefore, she is the major reason I picked up my accent. So, I spoke English-Turkish and Arabic at home, and English and Arabic at school with my friends.

Having graduated from high school, I went back to Turkey for my degree (ELT), and by the time I was back, I was fluent in speaking my mother tongue yet had lost my fluency and accuracy in writing Turkish. I did manage to improve but, until today, writing an email or texting in Turkish is a great burden for me, I prefer English. Speaking about the university, I remember one day when I was sitting and chatting with my friends in Turkish and we had a bunch of Lebanese guys talking about us, how 'pretty she was' and so on. They were speaking Arabic and, as I understood everything they said, I asked them to join our group. My friends were shocked, the guys were shocked, but we have been friends ever since. In fact, one of the guys is my husband today. :D So speaking more than one language is powerful!

As years passed by, I lived in Turkey, where I was mainly exposed to Turkish, but then I moved to Spain, where I fell in love with the language. When we moved to Madrid, I started learning Spanish through courses, listening to podcasts, and songs, and watching movies and series, and now I can say I am at a good level of Spanish. I can even understand the different accents from different countries in South America. Although I am not a very fluent speaker of Spanish, being able to identify these differences makes me extremely happy. Speaking different languages, I feel creates a multifaceted identity. I think it made me an adaptable and dynamic person in society and speaking and understanding these languages gave me self-confidence. Also, as self-expression is different in many languages, speaking these languages made me understand my emotions and feelings better.

Hazem (a young man born in Morocco)

My journey in learning languages and becoming plurilingual dates back to my early childhood when I got in contact with my mother tongue, Darija. At the age of five, I joined a private primary school where I started learning standard Arabic and French. I still vividly remember my first subject there; it was a French language class. At that time, I did not understand a single word and I felt like an Alien visiting earth for the first time. However, by the time I reached sixth grade, I had become fluent in both Arabic and French.

In the seventh grade, my parents decided to enrol me in the American Language Center of Marrakesh, since English was taught only from the ninth grade. Learning English there was fun and entertaining, and it made language learning easy for me. In addition, French helped me a lot in the process of learning English. However, it was unlikely to find a context where to practice the language outside the center, so I joined a drama club, but I did not enjoy it and quit after two months. Instead, I started to print American rap music lyrics and memorize them, watch movies and series with subtitles, and chat with teenagers from all over the world in English to improve my language skills. After learning English for five years, and getting my baccalaureate, I was ready to take the TOEFL test and start learning English at university in Marrakesh.

Unexpectedly, however, I decided to embark on a new challenge and travel to Russia to study medicine and immerse myself in a new language, identity, and culture. I have many anecdotes and funny moments of the first three months. Since I only knew the words 'Da' (yes in English) and 'Niet' (no in English), I had to use them to answer any question asked of me. For example, when they asked me 'What is your name?' I answered 'Da'; if someone in the market asked me 'How many items do you want?' I responded 'Niet'. I could hardly find someone who spoke English, so I started to take Russian classes, make Russian friends, listen to Russian music, watch Russian movies, and get familiar with Russian culture and traditions. I found myself more focused on learning Russian language and culture more than on learning Medicine. Later, I worked in a night club for two years, then in a bar for two years, and finally I worked in a restaurant for one year. My purpose was to intermingle with the locals and be a part of their social group, and I succeeded. Over the course of seven years, I made a myriad of Russian friends who often called me 'the Russian'. As a result, I failed in my studies but succeeded in acquiring a new identity.

Then I returned to Morocco, where I began the journey of rediscovering and practicing my original identity. A year later, I decided to pursue my old plan of advancing in English studies. Even though I had not practiced English for more than eight years, I plucked up the courage to enrol in Marrakesh University. My experience served as a catalyst for me to work hard and stay determined. My current station now is Madrid, the opportunity to learn a sixth language, and become a polyglot. Nowadays, in my free time, I use YouTube and online translator sites to learn the Spanish language and culture. Moreover, I go out with Spanish friends to visit places in the city and practice the language. Meanwhile, I keep practicing Darija with my family through video-calls and bimonthly visits. But Spanish will not be my ultimate language to learn, as I am planning to add Chinese to my linguistic repertoire.

Nubar (a young woman born in Azerbaijan)

My language journey is not a very complicated one. Since I can remember, I have been exposed to two languages at a time, both Azerbaijani and Russian. But one that dominated the household the most till I was 6 (before going to school) was Azerbaijani. We lived in the same block with my grandparents and the only mutual 'lingua franca' with them was my mother tongue. Furthermore, all my relatives (excluding my parents) knew only this language for communication. Acquiring Azerbaijani was a natural process for me. Afterwards, one of the pivotal moments was when my mom started working so, for me not to be alone, she hired a nanny, who had only one requirement, to talk to me only in Russian. So, I was not only exposed to Russian books or games but, most importantly, to Russian cartoons. No doubt that those cartoons helped me shape as a person and obtain a lot of knowledge that I am also willing to share with my future kids.

Learning Turkish always is associated with fun times for me. Singing and dancing were an inseparable part of the learning process. After the fall of the USSR, Azerbaijan and Turkey became closer than ever, which resulted in good trade for both sides. Hence, Turkish series, films, songs, and artists were on every TV screen of an Azerbaijani house. Whilst watching and listening to all the exciting things on TV, not only did we learn the language, but it also helped in strengthening the relationship between the two countries. Years passed, and I find it interesting that even though Turkish is not a language that I am incredibly efficient in, I believe my association with the fun times that I had whilst being exposed to it has made me always find Turkish humour exceptional. In fact, I gladly admit that Turkish formed my sense of humour.

The next language I was exposed to was English. It all started with my mom's unrealized dream of becoming an English teacher. Being born in the years when USSR still existed, made a huge hurdle in the English learning journey that she wanted to indulge in. I remember her telling me stories about what hardships her father had to go through to find books that were not sold in Baku (the capital) and what joy it brought her to study those. Unfortunately (or fortunately), after marrying my dad, she chose to be fully committed to the role of 'the best mom in the world', resulting in her refusal of career opportunities for many years. Naturally, after so many years of not using or practicing the language, she lost almost all of it but made a promise to ingrain that love to her children. And that absolutely happened.

Since I was a child, I would play with my dolls as if I was teaching them something. And on one beautiful day, my mom decided to enrol me to English classes near our house. That was the day I fell head over heels for the language. It was truly love at first sight. And that love made me realise that, for me to be happy in life I just have to combine the two things I love the most — 'teaching' and' English'. I remember talking to tourists was the apex of the day!!! Since it was the only way, I could show off my mom the skills that I've come to learn. So, I believe, it was a 'win-win' for both of us. However, one episode of my life I deem to be very unpleasant, was when my grandparents gathered all the relatives together and made me and my cousin (the same age as me), speak in English in front of all of them. I remember exactly how uncomfortable and scared I felt at that moment. Now, reflecting on those days, I understand why speaking English in school, in front of my classmates, was such a horrifying practice to me.

Other language narratives

Other inspiring narratives written by renowned linguists who discuss their lives and their languages are available in the book *Language and culture: Reflective narratives and the emergence of identity*, edited by David Nunan and Julie Choi. Further personal experiences of language, both in oral and written form, are available here:

https://www.open.edu/openlearn/education-development/education/english-personal-experiences

https://www.firstlanguages.org.au/news/languages-and-me